A BIRD'S-EYE VIEW

AN ANTHOLOGY OF ESSAYS

A unique perspective on socio-economic and political issues with an abstract touch.

ADITYA BIHANI

Notion Press

Old No. 38, New No. 6
McNichols Road, Chetpet
Chennai - 600 031

First Published by Notion Press 2020
Copyright © Aditya Bihani 2020
All Rights Reserved.

ISBN 978-1-64899-607-8

Contents

Introduction

What is this book about?

It is a collection of essays on contemporary Indian and Global issues. Divided into three distinct sections with a total of 14 essays of varying length, the book aims to provide the reader with a wholesome exposure to ideas surrounding political, economic and social sciences. This collection of essays does not belong to any one genre or field but is a mix of the existential and the abstract. Explanations often accompany jargons when used. I refrain from explaining what each essay has in store for the reader, simply because every piece follows a brief catechism of the same.

Many pieces are inspired by ongoing events or the general state of affairs at a given time and hence, each essay is accompanied with the date of completion so as to provide contextual relevance.

Inspirations...

This book is inspired by intellectuals who dare to support reason in the face of widespread ignorance. I personally consider this book to be an addition to the literary legacy created by paragons such as Amartya Sen, Shashi Tharoor and Ramachandra Guha. This book is inspired equally by my mentors, teachers and professors, who have been pillars of constant guidance and support. And lastly, but also most importantly, inspired by my grandfather and mother to whom I credit my existence and achievements.

Purpose of the Book...

Education: the Indian system needs a practical approach and this work shall serve as an attempt to connect theory to praxis. This book represents the collective unheard voices of many, who due to societal or political restrictions fear expression.

This book is a tribute to the journalists and intellectuals who dare to raise their voice in dissent. This book is a tribute to every dedicated teacher and to all those who strive towards advancement and progress. This book is a tribute to all who believe in the power of thought and reason, and in its spirit do not cower in the face of argumentation.

An important aspect to keep in mind is that these essays are an effort to present my perspective (which admittedly isn't entirely unique, but a mix of many others; for that matter no perspective can be unique in its entirety); a perspective which many may agree with or not. Disagreement is welcome and so is criticism. Keeping in mind the importance of scrutiny, which is what this book stands for, I am open to opinions and arguments. I have tried my best to be as accurate as possible as far as factual statements are concerned, however as humans we do tend to make errors. Please do point them out and reach out to me. (Contact details are mentioned in the end).

Section

1

A GLOBAL PERSPECTIVE

This section is a collection of essays on the largely unfortunate state of the global economy. There always exists hope, however being unaware of the predicaments that plague us at an international level is a blunder one cannot afford to commit.

1. Peasants and Pitchforks
2. A Possible - 'Russian Spring'?
3. Protectionism: Smart Economics OR Vote Bank Politics?
4. National Interest VS Global Interest

1

Peasants with Pitchforks

Prabhat Patnaik in an article mentioned the likelihood of contemporary fascism, which would rise to balance the persistent inequality. Talking of fascism, let us look at the political trends in a few of the major powers of the world today.

"The rich have got to fear the peasants with pitchforks" a dialogue in the famous series "Fargo" resonates the nuclear thought of a "Worker's Revolution" in Karl Marx's Magnum-Opus, the "*Communist Manifesto*". The prevalence of such a credo has been gaining ground as of recent times. Increasing capitalism and its self-serving ideologues have successfully thrown the blanket of an efficient free market system (citing advocates like Adam Smith and Milton Friedman) over their selfish pursuits. Arguments in favour of capitalist interests are those of increasing employment and the percolation of wealth down the economic pyramid, which are however today facades under which lies its greatest gremlin - INEQUALITY. Inequality is ever increasing and ironically so even in countries, such as China, which ironically are communist regimes founded on socialist principles of which equality is quintessential. Such profit mongering has indeed become life-siphoning, resulting in widespread discontent; the Yellow Vests Protests in France are a case in hand.

Increasing trends of authoritarianism observed in nations which were/are emblematic of freedom and liberty is indeed distressing. A survey by "*The Economist*" on the democracy index has seen the United States being labelled a flawed democracy, which has taken several on a tailspin. The irony in The United States' almost anti-global and anti-diversity regime led by President Trump (we've heard President Trump's views on "shit-hole countries" and are seeing his "America first policy" come in strongly) is how it is digressing from the gauge it once set by giving impetus to globalization and liberalization, which started with the Marshall Aid to devastated European countries.

The Indian Modi-led government and its tenets - pseudo named by Shashi Tharoor in his recent book "*The Paradoxical Prime Minister*" as "Moditva" (or "Modi-ness") - seem to be swaying the Indian society away from its secular socialist doctrines. This compounded by the inherent pluralistic nature of the Indian society strengthens the need for us to NOT embrace authoritarianism and admonish on our rulers this very demand.

Today, Communist regimes such as China are evolving into freer market structures with Entrepreneurs like Jack Ma serving as beacons to the emerging middle class. This is necessary for the establishment of a much required circulation of elites known as the "Schumpeterian Entrepreneurial cycles". This democratizing trend is however threatened by developments such as the scraping of presidential term limits, making President Xi Jinping a lifelong ruler, much like archaic imperially unchallenged monarchs. The situation is further exacerbated by inflating inequality in China as well. The current billionaires such as Wang Jianlin are self made, yet their children spare no worry in showcasing their billion dollar lives. Such showcasing can indeed serve as triggers to suppressed agitation (regarding the idea of being born with a silver spoon); which would have been fine in itself; however the fact that this silver spoon comes at the expense of the common man's "bronze" spoon (or no spoon at all) along with bragging about the same can be hurtful.

Russia led by Putin is in no better a position. The Russian elections seem farcical with the same individual being elected president in alternative terms, only due to legislations that demand so. The framework which requires that no individual hold presidential power for two or more consecutive terms (to prevent any sort of authoritarianism, which could possibly arise from a continuous rule) has seen itself being fooled by the alternative term agenda. Russia is indubitably an authoritarian regime.

Brazil's recent appointment of Jair Bolsonaro as president is discomforting given his disposition as a homophobe and as a believer in war and torture (in view of past statements and records). Awaiting Brazil is a future with high uncertainty and anxiety. Will this incumbent take Brazil to further heights, using its massive potential as an agricultural giant in the globe or will he give rise to the likings of Stalin's Purge. The favelas in Brazil call for attention, but only time can tell if they will gain support.

Such trends towards authoritarianism seem to be fulfilling Patnaik's predictions. All of such leaders promise freedom from oppression and despair. They promise a "flatter world" with minimal inequalities (at least in terms of opportunities). However history provides a contrasting and controversial narrative; one which portrays such leaders as nonchalant and ignorant once in power (and rightly so, for recorded history is no myth, nor is it a fairy tale, but it is the bare truth). As Charlie Chaplin in his "*The Great Dictator Speech*" rightly says - "By the promise of these things, brutes have risen to power. But they lie! They do not fulfil that promise. They never will!".

The need for the day is not to rise with pitchforks against the rich, but first to rise against fascism with libertarianism, and against any move towards totalitarianism with democracy. Let's not give into a system which steals from us our right to voice and decision. As Amartya Sen and Jean Dreze mention in "*The Uncertain Glory*", of Democracy even if flawed, providing at least the right to decide one's leader (the imperative tool of anti-incumbency). Raghuram Rajan, wrote in one of his earlier articles about the pillars of a democracy and its efficacy; the four pillars being: 1. Electoral Competition, 2. Checks and Balances, 3. Rule of law and 4. Prevalence of Free Markets. Had Mao faced these four pillars, the Cultural Revolution may never have to come to pass. The gift of benevolent dictators like Lee Kuan Yew is as scarce as hen's teeth and can barely serve as an argument, if one at all, to give a window to an authoritarian regime.

"Let us fight to free the world - to do away with national barriers - to do away with greed, with hate and intolerance. Let us fight for a world of reason, a world where science and progress will lead to all men's happiness. Soldiers! In the name of democracy, let us all unite!"

– Charlie Chaplin's
"The Great Dictator Speech"

2

A Possible - 'Russian Spring'?

Andrea Asani's paper on the economic motivations of the Arab Spring elucidates how a grave amalgamation of unemployment and wealth inequality, resulting in relative deprivation, quite logically culminates into a much desired uprising; the need for which gained greater importance given the absence of a democratic construct in the "Arab Spring" countries which were moving towards a neo-liberal capitalist regime since the 1980s (with the Nasser regime).

Do we see a similar trend in Russia? Will Russia undergo a revolution similar to the Arab Spring? Let's discover…

This piece was completed on the 1st of April, 2020.

The Arab Spring is one of the most tragic yet propitious events of the century. The MENA (Middle East and North America) countries, subject to grim despair and in a state of dire disrepair, did call for a much required systemic change. The overhaul of the prevalent economic and political construct required an uprising of a magnitude no less than the "French Revolution".

Anarchy develops from utter discontentment amidst the masses with alternative political ideologues fuelling the arising insurgent fervours. Discontentment often emerges from factors rooted in prevailing economic institutions.

The economic problems observed in the Arab Spring countries draw parallels with the existing scenario in Russia.

Even though unemployment figures (as low as 4%) in Russia portray a healthy image, the same is an outcome of forced employment, which has been a classic Soviet Union tactic. However these figures are farcical for reality is mirrored in the excessive prevalence of underemployment and disguised unemployment compounded with a spike in temporary job numbers. On other side of the funeral pyre, we also had the Arab Spring countries suffering massive unemployment, which was however an offshoot of a youth bulge and the absence of skilled-job opportunities.

Russia broke out from a communist setup with the collapse of the Soviet Union; Mikhail Gorbachev introduced the "glasnost" and "perestroika", a move away from communism. Russia much like Egypt in the "Nasser" regime looked towards international citadels of liberal thought for guidance. This was an opportunity that appears rarely; a chance for economists to check the viability of neo-liberalism in a nation geared to metamorphose. The experiment seemed to prove the futility of a quick neo-liberal transition in the absence of slow and impactful institutional changes that would have constructed a favourable milieu for such a transition. A research paper by David M. Kotz illustrates the eclipse of the Russian state as it succumbed to the Gordian knots of this new regime; Russia's GDP had tumbled to half in the period 1991-1998 with investment sentiments degrading further which was an appendage of the IMF-inspired tight monetary policy, making money so scarce that 70-80% of transactions were conducted via barter. The social condition suffered further dilapidation as it remained convulsed in alcoholism, suicide, murder, infectious diseases and stress-related ailments. Russia's transition to a neo-liberal regime resulted in the emergence of an oligarchic setup, an offshoot of crony capitalism.

This failed "neo-liberal experiment" should have been precedence enough to not have other emerging third world nations follow suit. However it is unequivocally not the current picture with developed and developing nations furthering this system by more deregulation as well as privatization.

Before moving on to the neo-liberal shift in the Arab spring countries let's discuss a few features of this system which tend to make failure endemic to the same:

- First, a lowering trend of efficiency and productivity has been observed in most nations with exceptions such as China, which still remain relatively regulated and hence not too "liberal" in its true sense.

- Innovation does take place but the same is as Thomas Pikkety rightly pointed out a "skill biased technical change" which when examined in combination with the Deepening of the Smiling Curve (the global value chain) would indubitably reduce unskilled worker output value added. This in itself is indicative of a higher proportion of income flowing to the capital owners and a meagre remainder left to be shared by the proletariat (who form the majority). It is ironical that in a democracy it is the majority that remains worse off.

- Making every nation a decrepit through an increasing inequality in income, which further transcends to excessive wealth inequalities and a vast gulf betwixt the standards of living between different economic classes.

- The oldest cogent reasoning given in defence of any capitalist system is the prevalence of the Schumpeterian entrepreneurial cycle resulting in a swift circulation of elites and hence preventing a stagnant unequal societal existence. This argument is an overtly idealistic one at best, given the rare presence of a "level playing field" (equal opportunities at every level) in most of the nations across the world.

To recapitulate, the world today is convulsed in neo-liberal capitalism which has over time resulted in the current "world capitalist crisis"; dampening of consumer demand due to stagnating real wages, compounded with unemployment and income inequality, defeating its primary virtue of innovation and private sector investment. One may ask how; well the logical flow is that a dampened consumer demand results in lower incentives for the private sector to invest, as no firm would produce more than the demand; even if they do so (to fill inventories), the multiplier effect of the same on the economy is minimal. Such an endogenous "crowding-out" effect is regressive for any economy. Furthermore, the current system of promoting deregulation increases excessive risk taking, which was the sine qua non behind the 2008 global financial crisis.

Clearly Russia did suffer the wrath of a neo-liberalism as did the MENA countries with the Arab Spring Revolutions. The future of the Arab Spring nations remains largely uncertain and unpredictable. A few coin it a failed revolution with the current state much more tragic than its past. Yet there do exist an optimistic few, who render the current state as a quasi-authoritarian limbo, wherein the remains of an old system form a hostile institutional environment for democratic reform efforts. To study Russia through the lens of the Arab Spring Revolution can be faulty given a difference in timelines, geography and culture, however Russia having not learnt and structured itself after the 1998 crisis does seem to be shifting towards an inevitable crisis analogous to the Arab Spring. The COVID-19 pandemic and its aftermath could further strengthen this possibility. The reasons to believe and perhaps reject this possibility shall be discussed presently.

The Russian crisis unlike others is enviable for it circumvented the prediction of a devastating cyclical fall. As for Russia, post its capitalist crisis of 1998, conditions were governed largely and quite literally so, by the then and current incumbent, Vladimir Putin. Putin's rise to power in 1999 was through a good network within the Russian oligarchy and military web. Making use of the same and further entrenching the same, Russia remains yet at large a nation in the hands of a few immensely wealthy oligarchs, who exist by "feeding the" and simultaneously "feeding off" the politically powerful. Thus Russia didn't as such undergo a systemic transformation in reality as much as it did on paper. Though unemployment rates reduced drastically, as they remain today, this was as mentioned earlier a classic Soviet Union tactic of "forcible employment". Similar state interventionist policies were adopted which on paper were indeed citadels of pure advancements, however in praxis remained unyielding given the expanding interface of corruption.

The public sector employment numbers rose by a quarter following Putin's election, yet lowering efficacy defeated the purpose of the same. There does exist a palpable prominence of a "Soviet-Nostalgia" in Putin's behaviourism and thought. Vladimir Putin began his rule in December 1999 by unveiling a memorial plaque to Yuri Andropov, who, as Soviet ambassador to Budapest, oversaw the invasion of Hungary in 1956, and who, as chairman of the KGB, established the Fifth Directorate, which was tasked with suppressing dissent and expanding the practice of "punitive psychiatry" whereby dissidents were committed to mental asylums. Early on in his presidency, Putin reinstated the music of the Soviet national anthem - personally picked by Stalin in 1944 - as the national anthem of Russia, and described the peaceful dissolution of the USSR as "the greatest geopolitical catastrophe of the 20th century". The retuned symbols of Soviet rule were quickly followed by Soviet-like methods of keeping a grip on society, from state control of television to the elimination of electoral competition.

However Putin's Soviet-ism suffers a massive internal hypocrisy. Though the oligarchs don't have half the power they had in the early 1990s, their existence still perpetuates given Putin's need for them. Further the autarch's rise to power in itself contradicts any true communist thought engrained in primordial Soviet thought. It is seemingly so that any effort by Putin to reinstate "Soviet thought" in Russia is to remain glued to the power he holds, much like Stalin. The international Russian image isn't appealing either, given the Ukraine conflict and Putin's rule, which has been labelled an authoritarian regime by

"*The Economist's*" democracy index rankings for quite some years now.

Furthermore stagnating real wages, rising inequality and massive underemployment results in a dampened consumer demand. A broader macro-economic outlook sees the Russian economy's dependence on oil exports as a "natural resource curse" having paved the way for the "Dutch Disease". The youth of the nation remain dissatisfied and as of recently people have observed a wave of insurgent fervour. This again much like every feature of Russian politics and society remains an enigma. Journalists across fail to reach a consensus on as to whether the Russian youth remain opposed to the overhaul of the current status quo or whether the youth shall penalize the incumbent in elections for the opaque and immoral form of governance.

In December 2017, the Levada Centre, the country's foremost independent polling agency, found that 86 per cent of Russians between the ages of 18 to 24 approved of the Russian president. Similarly, a poll conducted by the state funded Russian Public Opinion Research Centre (VTSIOM) after the presidential election in March 2018 showed that 67.9 per cent of Russian voters aged 18 to 34 cast their ballots for Putin. However on personally interviewing many youngsters in Russia, Dimitri Alexander Simes (a journalist and writer for "*The National Interest*") finds that the current incumbent does not go unchallenged by the youth. A major complaint is that Putin's unwillingness to step aside prevented a transition of power. "A president should not turn into a tsar, and the country under [Putin] is moving towards the time when there was a tsar," said Mikhail Sein, a Russian video-blogger and journalist. Thus though the picture is quite a conflicting and confusing one, it is not unknown that Putin tends to suppress any opposition, which could perhaps explain the approval polls by youngsters in Russia for such polls can at times be recordable and accountable.

The COVID-19 crisis adds an interesting dynamic to this issue. The coronavirus has yet to hit Russia hard. But when it does, as many experts soon expect, it could prove a huge challenge to Putin during a fragile time for his rule. Anything that distorts the image of Putin as Russia's hero, whether it is **large-scale protests**, a **prominent opposition leader** or **questions about his leadership**, will ruin the myth he and his allies have cultivated for decades. A significant COVID-19 outbreak in Russia, and particularly in the densely populated capital of Moscow, would be devastating to the dictator. A high death toll is distinctly possible, as medical resources outside Russia's major cities are scarce and the country's **older population** is at high risk. The looming crisis couldn't come at a worse time for Russia. **Oil prices**, the lifeblood of its economy, have tanked. Furthermore, the **transition plan to keep Putin in power** until 2036 has been delayed. And early data this year shows Russians are contracting "pneumonia" at higher rates than in the past; some critics say that it's actually COVID-19, and that **the government is manipulating statistics** to make it seem like the spread isn't that bad.

Put together, this is a "perfect storm of problems for the Kremlin", said Alina Polyakova, a Russia expert and president of the Center for European Policy Analysis in Washington. The stream of bad news had Putin hiding in the shadows, not wanting to take the fall for the deadly mishaps. But now that the number of cases continues to rise - and quickly - Putin has visibly taken command of the response. After all, he, more than anyone, is aware of the precarious moment in his leadership.

Thus a possibility of a "Russian Spring" is feasible, which would filter out any Soviet remnants in the Russian political construct and transform it into a nation with a responsible governance; in the presence of which a responsible capitalist or a welfare market economy can be beautifully yielding. However, the possibility of the same remains apocryphal given Putin's extensive and powerful reach throughout Russia. Unlike the Arab Spring countries wherein the monarchs were unable to anticipate the emergence of revolutionists and revolts which as dubbed by many were "leaderless revolts", Putin's Russia would not be easily susceptible to the same given Putin's excellence (and quite admiringly so) in the "Game Theory" of Russia (given his cautious and keen intuition on domestic occurrences and happenstances).

However on a much more ruminative note the need for a Russian revolution, is for reasons explained throughout, highly desirable. Russia needs to come out of its despotic shell and meet international standards on freedom and democracy. Its current bearing remains immensely regressive, which is a stance it can ill-afford. It needs to live up to the potential is has.

As Serhii Plokhy wrote: "The collapse of the Soviet Union, like the disintegration of past empires, is a process rather than an event. And the collapse of the last empire is still unfolding today."

3

Protectionism: Smart Economics or Vote Bank Politics?

In a world governed largely by free market dictums we are often made to acknowledge the largesse Globalization bestows on those who espouse its principles. As of recent, nations all across the world are resorting to protectionist or 'beggar thy neighbour' policies.

Is this paradigm shift rational economically or is there an underlying motive which remains invisible to the average netizen?

As of recent times tensions betwixt global superpowers has sent economies all over the world in a tailspin. With heightened uncertainty and volatility, growth seems to be dwindling in advanced as well as emerging economies. The Sino-American conflict has been gaining heat, with the U.S president 'Trumping' his "America First Policy" and China refusing to submit to American demands. It is indeed ironic to witness a nation (America) emblematic of liberty and freedom, take a radical stand in favour of protectionism.

Yet, as of recent, scholars and organizations have been working to discredit and disparage the duo of Globalization and Capitalism; a report by the UNCTAD highlighting the same is indeed difficult to deny, given its strong empirical support.

Donald Trump, who has been labelled impulsive, seems to be in favour of the view presented by the UNCTAD report mentioned above (the view is one against globalization and neo-liberal capitalism). However is his stance a reasoned and sagacious one OR is it merely an attempt to fill his vote bank? Let us try and discover the varied possibilities before us today.

A major argument by Trump, in favour of trade barriers and hence protectionism, is the loss of manufacturing jobs to countries like China. This reasoning seems faulty at best because the current secular decline of manufacturing jobs is a global phenomenon and not an American one. In fact making efforts to restore these lost jobs would be in vain, since our dynamic world - engulfed in the process of 'Schumpeterian Creative Destruction' - presents this dwindling manufacturing job scenario as inevitable. Advancing machinery and technology have indeed become a powerful wave which shall swallow any attempt made to hinder its flow; a wave which has purveyed humankind with wonders which were once only dreamt of; however such an opulence often comes along with a modicum of loss - which in our case is the dwindling number of manufacturing jobs.

Disrupting the flow of nature often results in a destructive process forcing a return to the primordial flow; analogously, Trump's efforts to inhibit the free flow of the markets would with time result in global economic loss (we are already witnessing the same) which would itself act as an internal force pushing it back on a path of correction till we attain a free market regime. However this transition would remain oscillatory at best so long as there remain opportunistic individuals who shall yet again resort to the "Trump Strategy" in order to gain populist support and fill vote banks.

The world today is deeply knitted in a web of global supply chains; so intricate that a tsunami in Japan could disrupt electrical production and supply in America (with Japan being a competitive supplier of semiconductor electronics). An imposition of tariffs by countries would ultimately result in a higher cost incurred by their natives both directly and indirectly. If one looks at a logical flow - if America imposes tariffs on commodity A which it imports from China, then as a result of reduced demand, Chinese production too would fall; now since commodity A is not solely produced by China (given the global supply chains), intermediate and raw material inputs from America and rest of world would in turn suffer a downturn; the end result being an overall deficiency for the global economy, with the gains never outweighing the losses.

At the same time however protectionism may not be as uneconomical as it may seem. Several scholars of the day are busy discrediting the neo-liberal capitalist system, of which free trade is a salient tenet. This movement against the right wing ideology has gained momentum, given the strong empirical evidence supporting their claims (the UNCTAD report 2018). With massive income inequality, implicit imperialism, waning consumer demand and stagnating growth, the need for a better market system does arise, in the process of which nations move inwards; in short adopting protectionist policies does appear reasonably rational.

Having explained the arguments put forth by protectionist ideologues and the possible flaws therein, lets now discuss an often neglected piece of this puzzle; a piece which is often the primary precursor to protectionism yet remains conveniently concealed behind the veil of national interest - **Geo-political motives and Strategic interactions** call for greater deference. The USA, with massive firepower and influential soft power, has for decades been the world leader; swaying public opinion and global paradigms it has grown accustomed to being referred to as the land of dreams and it dare not have China capture its hegemonic status. This supreme "image" that the United States possess has been a prime factor behind the opulence it relishes in. Despite its massive debt (around 200% of their GDP), it still commands investor confidence and Trump knows quite well that the citizens would try their best to prevent a dent in the image of the dreamy "American Dream and Saga". Thus it is not at all surprising to witness a slew of votes pouring into Trump's pockets as he promises to secure American credibility, influence and hegemony; protectionism is quite literally the empirical side to these promises. From a nationalist viewpoint, it does seem justifiable to have a president put the needs of his citizens before global ethics/interests, much a like a true sovereign, however efforts should be made to act more prudentially and to minimise losses.

Yet another interesting factor behind Trump's 'strong' threats and promises is the image of dominance and authority he builds for himself. America has witnessed a massive flow of immigrants over the years, which has often worked against the American lower middle income categories by depressing wages and lowering job availability. As such, if an individual (President Trump) who is supposedly 'one of their own' promises them their home and all of its opportunities, and presents himself as security or better yet insurance for millions of Americans who suffer the threat of losing their jobs to immigrants, it seems natural for the citizens to vote for him.

A recent study indicated that a majority of people across the world (America too) prefer an authoritarian leader, and Trump for sure has done due research and played this strategy well.

The Sino-American trade war is just one out of many instances of protectionism. India as of recent has seen the Modi government raise import tariffs/barriers (despite their disposition as a right-wing-free-trade party). With the upcoming 2019 elections and increasing demands for job security in a nation handicapped with unemployment, a move towards protectionism may seem as an easy solution to the ruling party. However we cannot afford to discount the economic damage caused by decades of import restrictions, which were dismantled under the Narasimha Rao Government in 1991. Accounting for the resurgence of right wing nationalism under the BJP, the shift towards populist protectionism becomes all the more probable, regardless the damage that would ensue.

A study conducted by Banri Ito, Associate Professor of Economics, Aoyama Gakuin University displays a strong positive correlation between protectionist declarations and the risk of anti-incumbency. In other words the greater the probability of a political representative losing power in an upcoming election, the greater are his inclinations towards appeasement and populism, which in turn becomes the raison d'être for protectionism. Banri, who uses Japan in his study, finds that: *"An increase in import exposure per worker in a candidate's constituency deters him or her from supporting trade liberalization."*

Having accounted for electoral pressure, Banri focused on three factors: incumbency, inter-cameral differences and vote margin. According to his research: *"The results of the respective regression analyses show that non-incumbents, candidates who run for the House of Representatives, and candidates with a low vote margin are more sensitive to import exposure in their constituency and, therefore, more protectionist. The results suggest that as the electoral pressure increases, politicians attempt to acquire votes by using trade shocks as a legitimate reason to advocate for protectionist trade policies."*

This concealed yet functioning link between protectionism and elections has been prevalent since earlier times, yet it is only now that recognition of the same has gained momentum. An earlier example of this is the tussle between America and Japan in the late 1900s concerning their automobile trade. Discomfort of American automobile production houses threatened by Japanese imports, was a source of concern for the American authorities, who then made efforts to construct implicit and inconspicuous trade barriers. These barriers in the form of VERs *(Voluntary Export Restraints - Japan would voluntarily limit their exports to America; the term "voluntarily" does in no measure encapsulate the truth behind this tool, for Japan was "forced" by America to "voluntarily" restrain exports, as America threatened to raise high import tariffs)* enabled America to satisfy domestic producers, whilst maintaining its image as an apostle of free trade; an incredibly smart move packed with deception.

With organizations like WTO it becomes difficult for any nation to go against free trade without legitimate reasoning; the test of legitimacy lying at the discretion of the WTO. Thus countries all over the world have come up with several non-tariff barriers to trade which seem innocuous and logical, however are deceptive and hurtful. Recent years have seen an irrefutable emergence of protectionism with non-tariff barriers to trade at the helm. This emerging trend is unlikely the result of "smart economic" decisions, but seems to be powered by "selfish power retaining" motives; motives which aren't based solely on the benefit of citizens, but largely pose as opportunities for political incumbents, effectively turning nations into flawed democracies and inefficient markets.

4

National Interest vs Global Interest

The debate between National Interest and Global Interest looms large above all countries today, especially the developed nations. Trump-led USA, following the "America First" policy clearly seems to give importance to the former above the latter. Officials cite multiple arguments to defend their stance, however criticisms are equally valid. The answer is not as simple as figuring out which stance has been more beneficial in the past. With evolving ideologies and advancing technology the answer to this debate would require an analysis of future possibilities.

This piece was completed on the 13th of December, 2018.

Frederic Grare's book on the geo-strategic dynamics existing between nations provides a comprehensive account on why actions taken by nations often seem to be in grave conflict with fundamental economic theories. A striking example is the trade relation between India and Pakistan. Even though both have immense gains to be exhausted, they seem to be in strife much more often than in tandem. The presence of exploitable gains itself demolishes any grounding for allocative efficiency to be attained between the two border sharing nations.

Politicians often validate the presence of such strife stating the need for national sovereignty/interests above global interests. Yet this is a peevish argument at best, one which commits quite clearly the fallacy of *petitio principii*. The true reason behind the ensuing conflict is an entrenched sentiment of hate and distrust one nation has for the other. This sentiment is positively losing ground, yet much remains to be done. Exacerbating this predicament is the regular use of this sentiment by Indian politicians to create fervour and gain popularity amidst the fanatic crowd.

Nonetheless the debate between National Interest and Global Interest looms large above all countries today, especially the developed nations. The Trump-led USA, following the "America First" policy, clearly seems to give importance to the former above the latter. The reasoning behind such a stance, as given by bureaucrats is one aimed at reducing the immense trade deficit it suffers with China. Although the reasoning may seem prudent, the consequences draw quite an opposing narrative.

A protectionist stance by the nation which formed the initial grounds for free trade (starting with the Marshall Aid) is bound to change perceptions, beliefs and ideologies throughout the world. A spiralling chain reaction could as well be anticipated. It seems highly unlikely that with the US assuming a protectionist stance, other developing nations wouldn't follow suit. Japan, which shares a positive rapprochement with the US, has done so by delaying its use of Chinese tech products (5G equipment) following the arrest of the CFO of Huawei. Such a stance should however be limited to developed countries (and perhaps China, which is almost a developed nation), as emerging economies like India would have far more to lose than gain given their excessive reliance on imports and the absence of an institutional as well as economic construct for self-sufficiency via industrialization in the short run.

However the idea of a chain reaction remains defunct in the absence of due deference given to the geo-strategic conflicts and tensions between the ruling powers. It is highly unlikely that Japan, China or Germany for that matter would be comfortable with the USA following protectionist policies. The possibility of such countries reaching consensus also seems highly apocryphal given that these nations would refrain from any harm to their export-oriented model; by doing something that would make others not want trade with them. (These Asian economies are showing signs of the "Dutch Disease" given their excessive reliance on exports to maintain growth.)

Protectionism exacerbates the modern financial crisis of dampening global demand and an increasing risk due to the provenance and proliferation of neo-liberal capitalism in nations across the world. Such a system increases the probability of a systemic financial crisis due to an increase in excessively risky ventures to maximize profits in a highly competitive milieu. This is analogous to the idea of "Minsky's Meltdown", which provides an explanation for the 2008 global financial crisis. This system also widens inequality with major portions of total national earnings flowing to CEOs, investment bankers, entrepreneurs and "lucky" stock investors whilst the real wages of the middle class remain stagnated in most nations, whereas in other nations real wages are increasing marginally. We witness a "hollowing of the middle class". What is further distressing is that such inequality creates an image of risk being in direct correlation with profits and thus pushes more people towards the same process, furthering this perpetual cycle.

Marx saw the capitalist system suffering an endemic failure. Adam Smith would perhaps be more accommodative, however the neo-liberal capitalist free market system that exists is far from being the haven of efficiency and productivity he would have envisaged. Along with dampening global demand, productivity and efficiency are seeing the lowest rates of increase in the recent decades. This results also in a reduction of investment, as supply in excess of demand is futile to the producers. Therefore innovation, which is the primary benefit of such a system, can barely take shape and form with reduced investment from the private sector (crowding-out effect). With technology as advanced as it is today, a government can do almost nothing to augment innovation in the absence of an active and motivated private sector.

Protectionism inherently seems to always end in a systemic failure due to slowing efficiency, productivity and innovation. This shall yet again result in the prospects of a free market regime, however the brunt of collapse shall be borne by third world countries, which would then bear the trade deficits as developed nations run a trade surplus. In this "zero sum" game the rebalancing, which nations seem to want, is not in any way assured.

Prabhat Patnaik talks of a regression of the current world system towards the old colonial-like setup wherein one-way (not bilateral) trade existed. Colonists like the "British Raj" dumped their goods in the Indian (and other colonies) market by maintaining negligible import tariffs in India along with high import tariffs in England (thus preventing Indian exports from gaining ground). Today, the stance and principles behind the US protectionism are similar, one driven by a need to maintain a trade surplus. However what is worrisome indeed is that such a stance in the colonial past could well be anticipated given their inclination towards mercantilist thought and the very fact that countries like India were "forcibly handicapped", however in the modern era, with globalization and liberalization having taken off, ideals like those mentioned in this statement are condemned and not condoned.

The path for India seems bleak, given its disposition in the world as a nation heavily reliant on energy imports. Volatile foreign funds in India, as a few call "speculative hot money", exacerbates the uncertainty of events that lead to currency depreciation, which could widen further the deficit and also cause inflation due to increasing import prices. We need to progress, yet the government seems nonchalant. Major developing nations are taking salient steps to gain prominence both economically and geo-strategically, giving them greater bargaining power which tilts the terms of trade in their favour. India should do the same. Prudent governance and a healthy private sector can make India the next global superpower. India should maintain terms of free trade just as all nations should. America is suffering from a Trump syndrome which will lose heat as soon as he is out of power. Yet the question that stands is whether America will remain the global superpower throughout Trump's term in office. Famous for his impulsive policy actions it seems only right to presume a graver protectionist stance from America.

However nations should be on the qui vive (alert) for such a stance and not be influenced by the same. Global Interest calls for greater importance than National Interest in a world built on globalization and liberalization. Breaking ties with those around you would result only in isolation and an autarky is proven worse than a free trade setup.

2

AN INDIAN PERSPECTIVE

This section is a collection of essays on contemporary India set against the backdrop of an evolving and unstable global setup. The last few years have seen India go through massive transformations; some of which have served to do greater harm. As India still struggles to recover from domestic shocks, worsening global markets undermine its ability to reach for the stars. This section discusses the varied issues that plague our nation and a few ways to navigate through the inevitable storm.

1. **An Uncertain Indian Story**
2. **RBI - "REGULATED? Bank of India"**
3. **Election Hysteria**
4. **INDIA - A land of contradictions…**
5. **Un-freedom of expression - an Indian predicament**
6. **It is time for India to revive *'Swadeshi'***

1

An Uncertain Indian Story

Recent developments in India draw a rather unfortunate picture. For a country which has the potential to surpass every other superpower in the world, we consistently underperform. The title of this piece is literally what it talks about - the unfortunate state of affairs which make our future more uncertain than ever.

This piece was completed on the 12th of January, 2020.

India has always been emblematic of tolerance and embrace. The Indian saga, quintessentially is a paragon of pluralism. The Indian identity corresponds not to any one single culture or creed but to a fusion of many, wherein every Indian is an ambassador of our multi-faceted, ever dynamic societal construct. Yet this lucid and beguiling picture is but quixotic, for it seems to be nescient of the past; a past which has often drawn a violent narrative of Indian pluralism. Recent developments, especially the COVID-19 pandemic, seem to augment this gloomy and chronicled narrative.

The pandemic has brought to light several structural handicaps that plague our country, especially healthcare infrastructure. However India is not the only country affected. A crisis of this nature is bound to take a toll on the economy, since all activity comes to a halt. The ramifications of this pandemic and the path forward are discussed in another essay at the end of this section. This piece focuses on the more structural and ideological problems that our country faces; problems which existed prior to the pandemic and will perhaps continue to exist after a vaccine is developed. If these problems remain unaddressed, India will continue to underperform even after the pandemic is over.

The current government (as portrayed by Prabhat Patnaik in his blog) has unfortunately indulged in "vilifying the intelligentsia". Exacerbating this threat is the oblivion most of us seem to live in. A narrow array of choices have been thrust on the voters. The opposition party is a choice no better than the existing setup, for Indian politics today is exemplary of a flawed system which exists solely to get to power and remain in power; with the politicians for some reason believing that a deviation from democratic, secular and socialist ideals (Nehruvian thought) is condoned once power is attained, for they shall supposedly correct the wrongs done when in power; which is in itself immensely dubious.

The Modi-led government has indeed won the hearts of a majority by promising a whole lot more dreams than they could have possibly fulfilled. Modi's prowess at addressing masses has been pivotal to his government's popularity. Delusive rhetoric has unfortunately won over reasoned thought (which remains direly absent in our current political setup). Parliamentary discourse is more often than not a session of unproductive whataboutery.

As fanaticism and bigotry gain ground the democracy index rankings have seen a downturn; increasing cow vigilantism with bare minimal action against it (apart from non-materializing promises) is slowly but effectively unearthing, the true underlying principles/ideologies of the current government, which are in flagrant conflict with those that they proclaim/acclaim to possess.

Apart from the ideological discrepancies, the government is as worse in the policy making/execution outlook.

The Central Bank in any democratic and neo-liberal economy (like India) plays a crucial developmental role. A coherence and concurrence between the RBI (Reserve Bank of India) and the centre is essential to carry out prudent policies aimed at tackling the handicaps of our economy. The rupee, very recently, started appreciating after a bout of depreciation which took the economy into a tailspin, resulting in increasing trepidation among the markets and households, ipso facto increasing difficulty in policy making. To attain a stable rupee and a swift economy, smooth cooperation devoid of schisms between the RBI and the centre is quintessential, however the current scenario presents a narrative quite to the contrary.

The government has for long now been a striking example of fiscal indiscipline. So much so that tensions between the RBI and the government with regards to austerity was pretty much anticipated with the upcoming 2019 elections. The RBI in its Monetary Policy Statements passed on Dec 5th, 2018 mentioned clearly the need to prevent increasing money supply in the economy given the mild yet possibly systemic inflationary expectations. It also mentioned a virtually closed output gap, which further bolsters the need for reduced government expenditure. A third argument for this stance is that, of a private sector, which requires stimulation after a dampening of demands, both internal and external, and hence a circumvention of the "crowding-out" effect that arises from increasing government expenditure.

However, governmental intentions to increase expenditure seem to display no signs of sagacity. This shallow move has become stereotypical of Indian politics wherein the government makes an effort to cover up the lags (of its long-term as the ruling party) by increasing expenditure excessively into productive sectors towards the end of the term and for some unfathomable reason, expecting the remunerations to be effective and wholesome; moreover this portrays their nonchalance to the predicaments that may follow by doing so. This trend furthers our political construct towards a flawed democracy.

A rise in crony capitalism; in conflict with the Nehruvian economic thought (on which was founded our economy) has the Indian structure faltering and the future seems bleak.

The only rescue are the emerging generations, who cannot afford to become sycophants of charlatans (which our country seems not to have a paucity of). The current scenario is emblematic of a self-perpetuating model, primarily because politics in India has become stereotypically entrenched as a corrupt and self-serving system, wherein exists no place for an intellectual with a broad-eyed view. This psychological factor is an unswerving threat to the success of the Indian saga.

As the youth of our nation, the burden of change and advancement of paradigms rest greatly on our shoulders. Let's not forget society as we pursue our economic *Amis/*pursuits for a 10 figure salary would be futile in a nation where your voice has no importance and where society has become a tragic debacle.

2

RBI - "Regulated? Bank of India"

There has always been a debate over whether central banks should have autonomy or not. A few argue that government regulation would help achieve congruence betwixt fiscal and monetary policies. However fear of moral hazard always exists - the government could always use their control to fund their populist and myopic goals. Empirical evidence suggests that autonomous Central Banks have achieved greater success in terms of stability and growth. India too has an autonomous central bank structure, however as of recent this structure has been under threat. Let's explore…

This piece was completed on the 16th of December, 2018.

The Reserve Bank of India is an autonomous organization aimed towards maintaining financial and monetary stability in India with its palmary task being inflation targeting. The RBI has over the years helped bolster economic growth by providing liquidity at the right time to the right sector, aiming for a moderate inflation of 4%. This is not to say that its actions are always prudent and prescient, however under the able leadership of Governors like Raghuram Rajan, our nation's central bank seems to have done a decent job. An imperative factor which has paved the way for its credibility and impressive repertoire is the prevalence of a functional autonomy. However in light of recent events, with the resignation of RBI governor Urjit Patel, this crucial pivot appears to be fading. This resignation **(as a result of disapproval against the government)** has been the coup de grace for the government's already ailing image **(the elections results so far seem to substantiate the same)**.

Shaktikanta Das, the new governor, has been the subject of massive scrutiny over the past few days, which should have been anticipated given the interesting turn of events. Many have stated his Master's Degree in History and not in Economics as the primary justification for his supposed inability. Yet, this is a faulty argument, which straitjackets one's credibility to one's degree by being ignorant to one's experience. This is not to say however that the academic field of expertise is irrelevant. Mr. Das an Indian bureaucrat has had experience in the political field which shall prove beneficial whilst making decisions at the helm of the Reserve Bank primarily because such policy making and implementation is not done on the basis of pure economic dogma; but by giving due deference to a political-economic flux, which is our Indian economy. Yet again the need for political expertise cannot be remunerating for a lack of economic and policy expertise, however Mr. Das' mettle, calibre and fortitude shall be put to test in the next few weeks.

An article published in "*The Economic Times*" on the 14th of December, 2018 by R. Sriram fends Mr. Das from the criticism heralded at him over the past few days. The write-up is a highly spirited defence, yet, to simplistic, devoid of certain details which if accommodated would turn this defence on its head. An effort to accommodate such details should not be misunderstood as a distrust I hold against Mr. Das, for we cannot afford hasty generalization in an era where it's all the more prominent **(quite unfortunately so)**. This is an honest effort to try and understand a more complete and wholesome argument.

The article by R. Sriram is available at:

https://economictimes.indiatimes.com/markets/stocks/news/this-isnt-sparta-why-das-may-succeed-where-patel-failed/articleshow/67085679.cms

Sriram begins by stating the need for effective communication between the RBI and the central government given the fact that the latter is the largest stakeholder of the former. This is indeed much required given the role of the state in developing the economy via fiscal intervention. However communication is in no way implicative of acquiescence, for this would demolish the essence of autonomy forcing accommodation of every fiscal need, which in turn would be inimical to growth.

Sriram accuses Patel of turning a deaf ear towards the government, when in truth all he did was not knuckle under the inexorable needs of the state. The primary fallacy of this first argument is the fact that if Patel didn't consider government voice, then there would have been no disapproval or fallout between them. Whether, Patel's not adhering to government prescribed ways is right or wrong is yet another gambit and shall be discussed presently.

The RBI recently released its fifth bi-monthly Monetary Policy Statement 2018-2019, substantiating its stance of calibrated monetary tightening **(which means that there exists no possibility of a decrease in interest rates in the future, with the current/revised interest rate same as before. Also keep in mind that a lower interest rate is indicative of an increase in liquidity)**. Food prices though low currently, are expected to rise in the future given the predictions of a scant rainfall. Core inflation **(inflation of all goods leaving food and fuel)** is already high at 6.1%, far above the desirable 4%. The very recent jump in oil prices **(with the OPEC reducing supply of oil by 1.2 million barrels per day)** is bound to increase transportation costs and hence production costs, with the trickledown effect ultimately raising inflation. The service sector is healthy and furthers a rise in prices. The MSP (minimum support price) and HRA (house rent allowance) revisions will also soon pressurize prices levels toward an increasing trajectory. Such possible inflationary trends have to be tackled via a tightened monetary stance, which is what the monetary policy committee under Patel sought to do. It is disturbing that Mr. Das, soon after becoming the Governor, projected a dovish stance **(one who would not mind lowering interests rates and hence increase liquidity),** which is in dire contradiction with the ensuing RBI stance and statement.

What is all the more interesting is that an increase in liquidity in an economy suffering from a credit crunch **(due to the defaulting IL&FS - Infrastructure Leasing and Financial Services)** is precisely what the government wants, given its desire to raise market optimism and hence woo the voters towards their vote bank. Thus there does exist an uncanny parallel between the ideologies of the state and those of Mr. Das. This is again expected **(ironically so)** given Mr. Das' great understanding of the inner working of the finance ministry. As Sriram mentions, "He knows PMO officials and most definitely would have a good understanding with [then] finance minister Arun Jaitley." (Arun Jaitley passed away on August 14, 2019 and at present Nirmala Sitharaman is the finance minister). Given such a rapprochement between Mr. Das and the finance ministry, the resignation of Mr. Patel with Mr. Das becoming Governor would be seen by many as typically a strategic effort by the government to have the central bank in its pocket.

Sriram talks of "The government being the most important stakeholder" and the "most important player of the day". The importance of the government is indubitably pivotal however this does not imply that its decisions at all times and all situations are prudent. Furthermore given the current government's inability to fulfil its unrealistic commitments, compounded with the poorly performing economy of the day does raise a massive shadow of doubt over the government's decision making capabilities. Furthermore the cronyism prevalent in the BJP's policies shout out loud of similar objectives in the upcoming stances and decisions. Thus Sriram's argument of accommodating the states' voices and needs would stand logical had our government been all the more moral and sagacious.

The fallout between the two was primarily due to a disapproval of the RBI to provide fund reserves to the government. Our government, which is typical of a spendthrift when its term is close to an end, can distort the already volatile stability of our Indian economy. Increased government spending at a time when the "output gap remains virtually closed - (RBI statement)" could result in an inflationary spiral. More detrimental would be the act of encouraging such course of actions as it would engrain furthermore the behaviourism of procrastination and later redeeming oneself via excessive spending, whilst being deliberately nonchalant towards the massive fiscal deficit.

What the government desires is an overtly accommodative RBI, which could quite assuringly lead to hyperinflation. History bears testimony to the same. Furthermore, increasing control over the central bank does draw a possible narrative of a probable situation where the Indian regime becomes a little like the regime of Zimbabwe under Mugabe, wherein the State coerced the central bank to keep printing huge amounts of money to satisfy its perennial demands leading to a tragic hyper inflating economy and uprooting entire societies. With the elections approaching, fiscal slippages and indiscipline are expected, especially at a time when our country simply cannot afford the same. However with the swap in the RBI governor, the possibility of fiscal indiscipline is no longer apocryphal for the BJP shall try its best to win votes in the states where it has yet not lost.

Farmer discontent and desperation is an important socio-economic issue which requires a detailed systemic restructuring. Though the current government promises debt relief and greater funds for the farmers **(which is why it demands greater liquidity)**, it seems likely that it aims yet again for a band-aid solution which amounts to almost nothing in the long run. This is what every government has been doing for years now, which reflects quite evidently in our ailing agricultural sector, which is excruciatingly underdeveloped in comparison to other emerging economies like Brazil and China.

In the very same newspaper with Sriram's article was another which proposed Vijay Mallya as a better candidate for the RBI

Governor. This satirical take of the current situation is also worth a read.

To conclude, I repeat, hasty generalization is not the way. Let's give Mr. Das the time he deserves to prove himself. However at the same time let us not be oblivious to the intricacies involved in such processes. The world where transparency is preached and proclaimed is ironically becoming more opaque with time. The need of the day is a wave of awareness, enlightening those in the oblivious dark. A world where knowledge is free and perverse seems not to fulfil its needs. This is not an attempt to discredit any writer or governor, but is an honest attempt, as a writer, to share a thought and possibly throw light on the obscure and ambiguous.

"Persistent questioning and healthy inquisitiveness are the first requisites for acquiring learning of any kind"

- Mahatma Gandhi

3

Election Hysteria (2019)

This piece was written amidst the anticipation and excitement that lay ahead of the 2019 elections. With each political party making promises which in realistic terms seem pipe dreams at best, this piece makes an effort to understand how fraudulent Indian election system has become - with false rhetoric and even more unreasonable promises, which post hoc always remain unfulfilled

This piece was completed on the 3rd of May, 2019.

Elections are sacred to the Indian Constitution for it remains a salient prerequisite for any functioning democracy. Today, this indispensable tool has unfortunately become a mere facade; one under which false promises raise temporary populist fervours to fill vote banks. This phenomenon, or rather should I say 'habit' has become a typical trait of the Indian political system. Jayati Ghosh, in a blog entitled "Cash for Votes Scam" portrays the very recent union budget (by the BJP) as explanatory of this ruinous 'Indian Habit'. The recent "interim" budget proposal is (and quite unlawfully so) in fact a "full-fledged budget" for it remains inclusive of tax reforms. Tax benefits compounded with immense government profligacy in the form of monetary farm support is clearly indicative of the ruling party's self-goal, which is retaining ruling status for the next term.

This self-goal is the primary "opportunity" for all political parties in every election. In fact, the obsession with this opportunity is unmistakably reflective in the imprudent ventures of political parties as elections near; an example of one being the fiscal deficit limit being raised to 3.4% at a time when the economic objective was to limit the deficit to 3.3%.

Claims from both sides targeted towards discrediting the other have become archetypical of Indian elections. With the unemployment figures appalling and economic growth losing steam, the very recent listing of Azhar as a global terrorist comes as a much required 'bonus' for BJP; having reflexively claimed credit for the same, the ruling party is making efforts to use 'patriotism' as a new weapon. The opposition in turn, like a true fighter, has flung back a slew of instances in which they themselves have helped remove terror. Yet in this hubris, our warriors in the election battlefield seem to have made a few errors, which I'm afraid shall remain irredeemable:

1. First, HYPOCRISY. No political party during elections should shift its primary agenda as and when evidence in support crop up. The mass political focus, of all contesting parties in the current election, has been shifting from economic growth, to unemployment, and now to terror as and when they receive new evidence in their support or against their opposition. This temporary attachment with a national goal is reflective of their nonchalance towards attaining the said goal. Terror is indubitably a national concern, but the question remains as to whether the ruling party would have played the patriotism card had Azhar not been designated a global terrorist. The opposition peevishly remains ignorant to obstacles which require systemic overhauling, but emphasize only on those which sway public sentiment in their favour. In fact the entire process of 'evidence' followed by a 'political stand' is faulty. It is evidence that should follow one's political stand so as to help gauge the credibility and weight of the stated 'stand'. However, it is unrealistic to expect one (especially political parties) to be ideally honest, yet at the very least one can expect humility, humanity and consideration. This takes me to the second error.

2. INHUMANITY. In the tussle for credit and recognition for the listing of Azhar as a terrorist, the mention of the lives laid down by several *'jawans'* (soldiers) in the political battleground remain absent. The leaders of our ruling party have made it a concern of praise for PM Modi, whereas the opposition is busy discrediting them for the same. What hurts me all the more deeply is that an incident involving the demise of our vanguards has become a political matter, whereas the least our

political contestants could do is be considerate and spare this incident the political touch. Please do not mistake this opinion as a submissive one devoid of a need for vengeance; an action to avenge lost lives is crucial, and a development has been made, but the same should in no measure be used as a political weapon.

Hoping to sway the imperial spectre into their hands, several smaller political parties like TRS have come to take an anti-BJP-anti-Congress neutral stand. They make similar promises, however their limiting 'regional/state' exposure does minimize any prospects of their ascendance. This is a good symptom in a large mess of ailments, which is the Indian political system.

As a ruling party, the BJP held leverage (last budget) via which it threw over the primary sector a blanket of support hoping to gain voter confidence. This action, exuding desperation, suffered a massive blow as scholars unearthed its inherent discrepancies. However the majority of the Indian population does remain oblivious to the same and are incredibly likely to make an uninformed decision.

In response to such populist moves, the opposition (Congress) spared no time in promising more populist and foolhardy proposals, an iconic one being the variant of the 'Universal Basic Income' scheme. Yet, Modi's charm and convincing rhetoric does sway the relatively poor in his favour.

A strong and effective opposition is essential to every democracy for it enables detailed checks and balances. Congress, the opposition party in India, is in no measure as effective as it is aggressive and impulsive. What should be a detailed, disciplined and progressive discussion in the parliament is in fact a heated quarrel amongst a majority of snollygosters; all of them resorting to tomfoolery instead of logical reasoning. The principal beneficiaries of every election are the parties that ascend to power and not really the citizens for the alternatives available to us are no better.

4

INDIA - A Land of Contradictions...

As we usher into the e-world, as we construct a virtual world with numbers and characters, as we replace the pat on the back with an illustrious emoji, we need to keep on the back of our minds that such progress should not be made at the expense of the Indian story.

The awe-inspiring Indian beauty moved a Mughal emperor to aver, "If there be a paradise on Earth, it is this, it is this, it is this."

This piece was completed on the 25th of December, 2018.

India has always been emblematic of a land full of embrace and acceptance. India's cultural opulence manifests through contradictions both subtle and obtrusive. Any truism about India can be immediately contradicted by another truism about India. It is often said "anything you say about India, the opposite is also true", and yet India is more than the sum of its contradictions. The world's largest democracy that is also home to the ageless caste system; a land steeped in superstition and spirituality which is a world leader in information technology; the nation of Mahatma Gandhi, the apostle of non-violence that is convulsed by periodic bloodletting - the paradoxes abound.

These seemingly onerous contradictions are truly boons in disguise for they account for the exemplary soft power India harnesses in our increasingly competitive global world. Apart from our mystifying history and mythology, soft power channels through Bollywood and the Indian cuisine. As a fact, the Indian food industry in the United Kingdom is culpable for more employment than their mining, ship building and steel industry combined

Thus the Indian soft power has always been in abundance, yet its efficacy was minimal till a few decades ago. Instead of having world influence, our nation was left dilapidated given our exploitation by several world powers. Thus an enigma prevails. The answer to which lies in Roosevelt's maxim - "speak softly and carry a big stick" - India only spoke softly and suffered from the paucity of sticks (as in hard power). It is only today that our nation, building an armoury of both the carrot and the stick, is amplifying the functionality of soft power.

India's embracing and tolerant nature was misused by the British to establish a Britain centered imperial setup fuelled and justified by their narcissistic idea of the "White

Man's Burden". After years of intense and broad exploitation; with the industrialization of England being premised on the deindustrialization of India; we were left dilapidated as well as impoverished and yet were, ironically so, overflowing with exhilaration as we gained independence; independence which was then even critiqued by a few as not being the optimum step given the circumstances.

Personally, I believe, that India's independence was more than just an outcome of a ferment, it was indeed an idea whose time had come and as Victor Hugo rightly said - "no force on Earth can stop an idea whose time has come". At the stroke of the midnight hour on the 15th of August 1947, "the soul of a nation long suppressed had found utterance"; the Indian identity was not formed but simply reaffirmed and reestablished.

The "Socialist Secular" India formed after independence, under the leadership of eminent intellects, did justice to its constitution as one based on democratic principles. However the economic outlook for the same was incredibly poor. Despite several development plans, India as an economy and a society underwent minimal expansion/development in comparison to what its true potential was. China and India for that matter started on similar platforms with resembling GDP rates (China in fact suffered the atrocities of Mao's brainchild, "The Cultural Revolution"), yet the difference that exists between the two nations today is incredibly appalling. The reasons behind several such deviances shall be discussed presently as a much required prelude to discuss - Which way now?

The five-year plans India had post its independence were exquisite pieces of work on paper but unfortunately did not crystallize in reality. As such the development of several public sectors were inadvertently overlooked. Education is the basis of a strong economy. Tagore rightly said, "The tower of misery on the heart of the Indian economy is the absence of an efficient education system." Post independence, we gave emphasis to the "basic education system" quite different from the "elementary education system" and took a lag as China along with the "Four Asian Tigers" took the lead.

Europe is home to the oldest educational institutions in the world; the first being built in Bologna at 1088 followed by the construction of several other citadels like the Ox-Bridge Universities. Thus it is seems fitting that Europeans have a broader and better academic structure today. Yet this discussion would be comprehensive only when we consider it in the backdrop of our rich academic past. Nalanda University is over 600 years older than any other university in the world and as legend has it "the number of books it housed was innumerable; with its library burning for three whole days when set on fire by Khilji". The enormity of the knowledge therein was immense and hence India being a humble abode to philosophers, mathematicians, astronomers and artists was a haven for learning.

The scenario today is quite to the contrary. Though we are much better off than what we were post-independence the scope for improvement is colossal. Today we have a few renowned institutes like the IITs and the IIMs, which are held in the same reverence as the MIT or Caltech, however given a complete outlook, education in India still remains an ocean of mediocrity with pockets of excellence. As we metamorphose from the clichéd India as a land of snake charmers into a land of software gurus and computer wizards, we need to bear in mind that a monumental effort is yet to be made.

Kaushik Basu mentions 'Nanritam' in an article as being symbolic of progress in this field. Nanritam, a non-profit welfare organization has established, the "Filix School" in the region where Jharkhand abuts West Bengal. This facility in structured on the Finland system of education, which is a world leader today. The model of Filix School deserves to proliferate. The modernity of this school is exemplary and it is encouraging to witness how well the youth of these remote regions are embracing it. With the advent of artificial intelligence and robotics, such an education will be critical. It is imperative for India that we spend time doing science and mathematics, instead of trying to show off the science and mathematics done 5,000 years ago.

On the economic front, even though our growth was quite slow - about 3.5% annually - for several decades after independence, this slow growth was a large step as compared to the zero-growth rate prevalent during the colonial times. The picture today is incredible given our growth rates far surpassing most countries in the world with a GDP which is the sixth largest in the world (having overtaken France very recently). However our per-capita GDP still remains excruciatingly low with India ranking 142nd.

Prabhat Patnaik rightly portrays in an article the overstated importance we shower over GDP; a hallowed acronym for every economist. Today exist several anomalies like India, which with a high GDP and a high growth, that remain unequal and underdeveloped societies. Therefore economists like Mahbub-ul-Haq (Pakistan) advocate social indicators as being a veracious gauge for economic development.

It is true that social indicators such as life expectancy, infant mortality, fertility rate, literacy rate or poverty level have become significantly better in comparison to its pre-independence levels.

Yes, India has in a way evaded the doom and gloom prediction as propounded by the "Raj" as they left our country and such an advancement is not easy to dismiss, but is this the whole story?

Evidently not. There are major shortcomings with breakdowns and thus an agreeable picture of a nation heralded towards development with justice would definitely not be a balanced account of what has actually been happening.

India has been much slower as compared to China in indicators such as longevity, literacy, child undernourishment and maternal mortality. In South Asia itself, the much poorer economy of Bangladesh has caught up with and overtaken India in terms of many social indicators. Even Nepal has been catching up now in the sense that it has social indicators similar to that of India's despite the former's per capita GDP being just about one-third of the latter's. Twenty-Six years ago India was the second-best in regards to such parameters among the six South Asian countries (India, Pakistan, Bangladesh, Nepal, Sri Lanka and Bhutan), but today is the second worst (ahead only of problem-ridden Pakistan). India has been constantly climbing up the slope of per capita income while stumbling down the ladder of social indicators.

The reason behind India's despairing development is the ineffective and flawed utilization of its exponentially increasing opulence (GDP); primarily due to the inefficacy of existing political/social institutions and the persistence of political clouts within. There is work to be done both in making methodical use of the fruits of economic growth to enhance the living conditions of the people and in reducing the massive inequalities that characterize India's economy and society. Talking of inequalities, let's look at the disparity within our country itself. States like Tamil Nadu, Kerala and Himachal Pradesh are far superior to the cow-belt region (namely Bihar and Uttar Pradesh) in terms of literacy and health care. Whilst many credit this to the relatively better conditions of the south during and post the colonial periods, a more accurate as well as comprehensive answer would be the difference in the political institutions and governance therein. Though corruption exists in both areas, the magnitude of the same is much larger and intense in the north than in the south. Thus if at all we want to progress, the solution would lie in addressing corruption and promoting accountability in our democracy, which shall be the next aspect of this essay.

Arrow in 1982 pointed out - "a truly selfish economy is bound to collapse". Corruption is centered around greed, which takes the form of self-serving and self-centered ideologies. If such vicious ideologies become a part of economic policies then the repercussions are bound to be devastating. Transparency and a removal of crony capitalism is something all political parties promote, but barely seem to bring it into effect. The 'Lokpal Bill', 'Anti-Graft Bill' and the 'Right to Information Act' are few measures to ensure transparency. We require many more.

Honesty is integral for a thriving economy, just as morality is imperative for an intimate relationship. Where factors such as honesty aren't naturally forthcoming (almost everywhere), we develop legislative, judicial and controlling authorities to offset the lacuna. However when these institutions fail to function smoothly, as in India, the outcomes are tragic. Thus amends need to be made to address the efficacy of existing political institutions in India that would having far reaching impact on the growth of our economy.

India has an impressive and indispensable democratic structure, however the presence of a few rough-hewn political hacks from the cow-belt region have made it into an unimpressive and unprincipled one. Undoubtedly these corrupt politicians are given the lion's share of the blame for India's distress, but we are also equally responsible for the same. There are multiple reasons behind corruption however the most detrimental is the trio of:

1. Informational lacuna - the very existence of asymmetric information which makes it simpler for those with greater knowledge to sheepishly fool and mire the unaware unto exploitation. Education is the tool to tackle this problem.

2. Social leniency - our tolerance and use of "lower-degree" corruption, whatever that means, results in an entrenchment of the same in our culture, making corruption an acceptable social behaviour. Changing our mindset and principles is the only rectification.

3. Prosecutional difficulty - strengthening the inner political machinery is the way to undermine such a shortcoming.

Despite our efforts to do away with such corruption there is always a reluctance and underlying the same is what we call an inertia of "social norms", and a belief that norms cannot change much until and unless some prominent prosecution with punitive judgment draws heralded attention to the transgressions involved therein. Thus if we carry on with our efforts, I am positive that we shall soon mitigate and eradicate much of our problems.

The public sector in every economy is one of enormous importance and given the crucial role it plays in the Indian development trajectory, it is particularly important to ask how the accountability of the public sector should be developed and strengthened. The centre of the public-private debate has always been the "need" of an expansive public-sector, whereas the centre of discussion should be "how" to operate existing public sector units, ensuring accountability and responsibility for those who operate such units.

Let's look at the power sector; seemingly progressive yet in comparison to China it remains inferior. The blackout of 2012 has become a blot on the repertoire of our public sector; the "Blackout Nation" as "*The Economist*" put it, needs to buckle up if it ever wants to become a haven for foreign investment and further technical development. A reason for China's public sector earning profits as opposed to the negative profits scenario in India is given as the greater scope of privatization in China. This is in fact a myth given China's superseding control over the energy sector in the country.

In India, the privatization legacy was initiated by the BJP stalwart Shri Atal Bihari Vajpayee and has been carried on to a great extent. However today this legacy seems to be losing ground, as the ruling government very recently shelved the privatization of Air India, a sick establishment which is becoming debilitating for our economy with every passing day. What every government needs to realize is that such policy changes (like privatization), which have been beneficial, cannot be forgotten, worse yet reversed. As long the "rulers" of our economy bear this maxim whilst acting India as a nation is bound to progress.

Yet another major challenge is that of employing all those millions of Indians who come of age and seek to enter the workforce every year but remain without jobs. It is not only imperative that the country grows at a pace that can absorb all job-seekers, but it must also expand activities that generate jobs whether in manufacturing or tourism (our fabled IT firms and BPO centres only employ a million Indians out of a billion). We are right to focus on the urgent need to upgrade our national "hardware" - the country's ailing infrastructure. But we must not neglect the "software" - the human capital without which no country develops. We must do much more to promote education, health care, and an end to caste and gender discrimination. Only then can we produce Indians truly ready to take India to the top of the 21st Century.

As we usher into the e-world, as we construct a virtual world with numbers and characters, as we replace the pat on the back with an illustrious emoji, we need to keep at the back of our minds that such progress should not be made at the expense of the Indian story. The story of an elephant with great understanding and tolerance towards all forms of existence, an elephant which is fast developing glazing stripes like the "Asian Tigers", yet remaining an understanding and wise elephant at heart.

5

Un-Freedom of Expression - An Indian Predicament

As we enter a new decade, the future of India seems bleak. In addition to the economic slowdown and nationwide discontent regarding the Citizen Amendment Bill, the freedom of our press is under threat, more than ever before. It seems that over the past few years, our press has faced increased suppression, which is contradictory to the essence of a liberal state.

This piece was completed on the 4th of January, 2020.

India has always been proud of its stature as a secular democracy. However, in the wake of the last decade, this pride seems largely misplaced. Freedom of the press is vital to the functioning of every democracy and is in fact symptomatic of the freedom that democratic dictums epitomize. This malaise extends to undermine the freedom of expression, which is pivotal to the existence of any inclusive and collective political state.

The crux of a democratic setup is the tool of anti-incumbency. This power that the citizens hold to overthrow a government which isn't functioning in alignment to the their needs, fails to lead to fruition if the citizens in question aren't well informed. Thus the existence of an informed base of voters is imperative and here is where the importance of our media outlets come in place. A majority of individuals rely on our press for information and with the latter not broadcasting the truth, either by force or will, we unfortunately end up with a pool of uninformed voters. Thus, the very essence of anti-incumbency loses its charm.

This year India fell two places on the global press freedom index to be ranked 140th out of the 180 countries, which form part of the evaluation. The year 2019 has been incredibly turbulent for our nation; with the economy struggling to regain momentum after the multiple whammy of demonetization, GST reforms and the abrogation of article 370. Growth rates are touching record lows; employment remains a major concern; our agrarian crisis and volatile food prices persist unabated. In the face of such predicaments, our Prime Minister's 5 trillion dollar promise seems bleak. Adding salt to injury is the dire state of our media houses. The press seems to turning biased and nonchalant. The ineptitude of our press is a multifaceted complication; a few facets of the same are discussed below.

The first facet is the increased investments by politicians and corporation in news media. This can serve to undermine the ability of our press to remain unbiased and potent. Unlike several democracies wherein political and corporate entities are restrained from holding media broadcasting and publishing rights, Indian media outlets are openly influenced by the same. For instance, CNN-IBN (one of India's biggest TV networks), and the group of regional channels, is under the control of business tycoon Mukesh Ambani. In addition to the bias that media has to their corporate owners, journalists are also unable to expose corruption charges of the politicians accused for they have close ties to the very same owners.

A second facet is the excessive dependence of local/regional media outlets (especially local news organizations), on government funding. Governments' advertisements for tender, employment notification and other aspects make up a lion's share of the total revenue for such small local news publications. As a result such outlets rarely criticize the governments' incompetence in fear that governments may pull out advertisements thus leaving their revenue stream dry. Excessive reliance of media outlets on advertisements by big commercial organizations plague our media platforms in a similar fashion. Ramachandra Guha in his book mentioned how organizations as big and reputed as the Tatas have been known to pull out advertisements from magazines and channels that have criticized their products.

A third facet is the ineptitude of journalists, who often function to support political agendas and motives out of fear. Politicians and often corporate entities seem to have these journalists well oiled; it is no wonder that we see several journalists supporting a few party ideologies. If politicians are unable to provide enough compensation, then dissenting journalists are often pushed to resign from their media houses. As a knowledge buff, I see only a few honest and informative outlets today, like small podcast houses and non-conformist journalists participating in the same that actually live up to essence of journalism. These small fountains of knowledge however have a very niche consumer base, thus not posing a threat to the government. As a result, such outlets thrive whereas any other influential media outlet attempting to the do the same would have its voice muffled. In addition, several writers, editors and columnists are often party propagandists or apologists; herein an ideology bias is given importance over the truth which is unacceptable for any journalist. One is free to express personal views, even tough or extreme, but it should not come at the expense of the truth, especially when the individual is an important constituent of our information/intellectual sphere.

A lack of free press does harm the freedom of expression, however there are certain aspects which add salt to this injury and thus undermine Indian expression to an unfortunately low level. In addition to the three facets discussed above, there exist a few issues that plague India, pushing it to the brink of non-original conformist expressional forms.

First, the pusillanimity of politicians is abominable. They bow down to bigots and fundamentalists, even if they don't share similar views; they do so keeping in mind only electoral considerations; they fear offending any religious sect, organization or community, thus often succumbing to the irrational wants of such non-accommodative groups. Cases in point are the banning of Salman Rushdie's "*The Satanic Verses*" or the exile of M.F. Hussain or the very recent controversy over Sanjay Leela Bhansali's movie "*Padmaavat*". Be it the Congress or BJP, both are exemplary of such electoral cowardice. In West Bengal, the communist leaders Jyoti Basu and Buddhadeb Bhattacharya had

Taslima Nasrin's books banned. Politicians are the least bothered about literary or creative freedom. This serves to stifle the process of innovation or criticism in the field of literature and art, since authors/artists fear backlash from non-accommodative social participants who, in the absence of a protective government, wreak havoc (which is a major task of any government in a democracy). Our governments are obligated to protect the interests of every group (minority or majority), however their actions clearly indicate a failure to do so.

The intelligentsia have always been paragons of reasoned thought and action. Labelling them anti-nationalists as and when they oppose populist policies is a regression toward pre-colonial blind conformism. In addition to the absence of a free press, suppression of dissent and scrutiny leaves the government largely unchecked; free to do as they yearn. Dissent is organic to the sustenance of any democracy and quashing the same leaves us with a system no different from a monarchy; the term 'ruling' party becomes all the more appropriate (their overwhelming majority in the Lok Sabha currently does give them a fascist 'ruling' authority). Talking of an overwhelming majority in the Lok Sabha, the government in power should understand the gravitas of the massive trust thrust on them by millions of hopeful citizens. Treating the intelligentsia like ignorant fools reflects poorly for a government which prides itself on rationality. Amartya Sen's writings often discuss the pivotal role dissent has played in the Indian Saga. Be it the mythical Ramayana, Akbar's royal rule or our anti-colonial freedom struggle, scrutiny, criticism and dissent have been fundamental pillars of reasoned social progress.

The issue of a lack of freedom of expression is an issue which remains undiscussed till one looks into Section 124A (sedition act) in the Indian Penal Code. This section is an unfortunate existence for it undermines the very essence of a democracy. I find its existence ironic, for it is a constitutionally valid tool which is incredibly unconstitutional. The Indian Penal Code defines sedition as an offence committed when "any person by words, either spoken or written, or by signs, or by visible representation, or otherwise, brings or attempts to bring into hatred or contempt, or excites or attempts to excite disaffection towards the government established by law in India". This definition whilst elaborate can still be misconstrued to include almost any actions which may simply hint at even a slightest discontent; the terms used under Section 124A like 'disaffection' are vague and subject to different interpretation to the whims and fancies of the investigating officers, hence leaving ample space for the government to use this as a shield against any form of criticism that may be authentic and legitimate. This section is a relic of colonial legacy and the British, who introduced sedition to oppress Indians, have themselves abolished the law in their country. There exists no reason for India not to abolish this section.

What did the Law Commission of India recently say about section 124A of IPC?

The Law Commission of India, on August 2018, published a consultation paper recommending that it is time to restructure or repeal the section of IPC that deals with sedition.

Dissent is some way or another has always been the precedent to any valuable social change. Be it the removal of 'Sati' (the gruesome ritual of burning the wife on the pyre of her dead husband) or our very own independence movement, dissent has been the prime precursor to all such vital social changes. When dissent is quashed, a nation regresses towards an archaic orthodox ideological state.

It is vital to remember that the current government is one with an overwhelming mandate, a full majority, not once, but twice in-a-row. For a government that seems to function unconstitutionally at best, I dare say Indians have misplaced their trust. Raghuram Rajan, a renowned economist and a personal idol, rightly says that checks and balances are an integral pillar to any functioning democracy, and thus, a freely functioning press becomes fundamental to ensuring the same. The lack of a free press is not only an infringement of a constitutional fundamental right, but is a disturbing symptom of fascism. In a period where fundamentalism and isolationism witness a resurgence, we need to stand out and live by our democratic dictums of pluralism as well as freedom of the press.

6

It is Time for India to Revive *'Swadeshi'*

As COVID-19 destroys lives and livelihoods around the world, and economies are forced into isolation, a new growth model needs to be developed. This piece is contradictory to the idea presented in the piece entitled "NATIONAL INTEREST VS GLOBAL INTEREST" in section I. This is so because the latter was written prior to the COVID-19 pandemic, which has wrecked the world to such an extent that the future is bound to entail a vast paradigm shift. This essay presents a possible path for India to recover from the pandemic.

(This piece is a publication of evolideas, an LLP which seeks to spread ideas and empower thought. I am privileged to be a founder member of this wonderful organization. The co-writers of this specific piece are Varun Nair and Devansh Singhal; both are editors at evolideas.)

This piece was completed on the 1ˢᵗ of May, 2020.

As our world hurls down a devastating socio-economic storm, reviving the *'Swadeshi'* movement is instrumental in insulating our country from global disruptions and rejuvenating its economic zeal. Initiated in 1905, *Swadeshi* was born to instil the spirit of nationalism in a colonized state and was influential in moulding the Indian independence movement. It gave a much required push to the domestic economic machinery, which, back then remained largely stifled by colonial shackles. In its economic aspect, the movement expressed a nationalist-protectionist sentiment against foreign capital and also manifested an outlook for promoting indigenous goods. In other words, *Swadeshi* was, and is, a clarion call of patriotic duty for people with capital and enterprise to pioneer indigenous industries even at the risk of small or no profit in the initial period. The rationale for a modern revival movement however differs from that of its colonial counterpart, primarily because India is presently an independent sovereign, and thus, is largely accountable for the disarray it finds itself in. The core principles of self-reliance, indigenous enterprise and mass participation remain fundamental to a modern *Swadeshi* revival and resonate with those of its pre-independence self. However absence of facets like a boycott of foreign goods and isolationism are the contours which differentiate this modern proposal with its historic counterpart.

The movement in 1905, was primarily aimed at stirring nationalism and hindering the colonialist's efforts to divide the nation further. Even though economic revival was a subservient motive, the movement did show signs of economic recovery. Today however, economic revitalization remains a major imperative for a *Swadeshi* revival. A major aspect to consider is the uncertainty surrounding the ongoing COVID-19 pandemic;

since there is no saying when this storm will settle, one needs to take measures accounting for the fact that our world may not be nearly as integrated as it was before. An impetus to boost Indian manufacturing across all sectors today is perhaps more integral, than ever. Prior to the COVID predicament we face today, every nation had a choice, to either integrate with the world economy and bear the fruits of globalization or to remain independent. The future however, may not prove to be one in support of global integration, and thus India needs to prepare for self-sufficiency, at the heart of lies the *Swadeshi* spirit of strengthening the "Made in India" agenda.

India in a state of despair…

The growth rate of the Indian economy has been on a downward trend since 2018, with the IL&FS crash which sent our financial system into a tailspin.

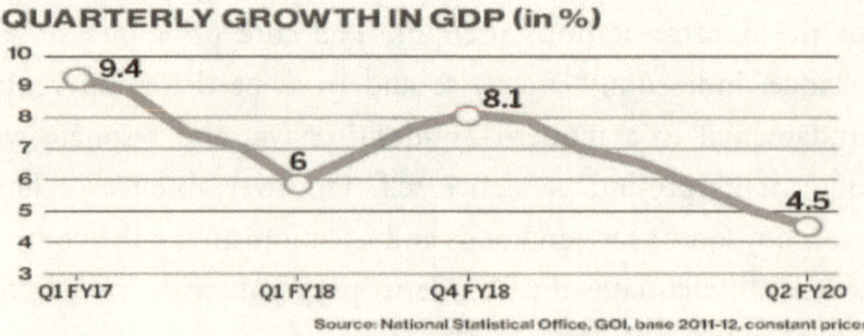

With the advent of COVID-19, growth forecasts all over the world are being slashed, and for India the growth rate cuts are despairing; International Monetary Fund (IMF) has cut India's growth forecast for FY21 in its World Economic Outlook (WEO) report from 5.8%, projected in January, to 1.9%; World Bank, in its South Asia Economic Focus report, reveals that India is likely to grow 1.55% to 2.8% in 2020-21; Moody's cut

India's GDP growth rate forecast from 5.3% to 2.5%. Lower growth amounts to decreased employment opportunities, which is bound to shoot up an already high unemployment rate; the overall unemployment rate may have surged to 23 per cent, with urban unemployment standing at nearly 31 per cent, amid the countrywide lockdown due to the coronavirus outbreak, Centre for Monitoring Indian Economy (CMIE) estimates showed.

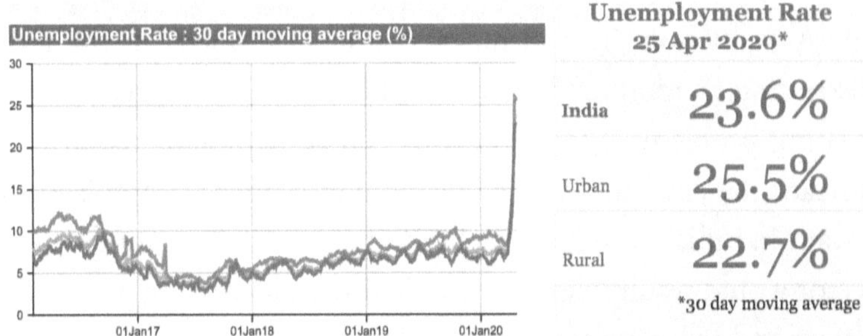

Source: Centre for Monitoring Indian Economy Pvt. Ltd. (CMIE Data)

India is however not the only one to witness dampening growth. Prior to the pandemic we witnessed a global slowdown, which according to many economists is largely a consequence of a major demand slump on account of structural problems; in other words the handicaps of neo-liberal capitalistic practices seem to be unravelling themselves. Consumer demand, which has always been the engine of growth for the Indian economy, is waning. Major reasons for the same are reduced purchasing power and an acute fear of what the future holds. The consumer confidence surveys conducted by the RBI have shown a dip in confidence which is why people are not willing to spend.

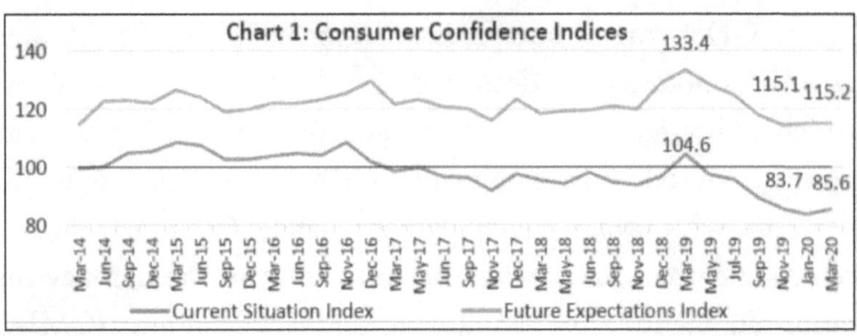

Source: Reserve Bank of India

A reduction in consumer confidence opens a far more distressing Pandora's Box of reduced investment, feeding into the existing problem of lower growth. These deplorable conditions warrant the need to revive a *Swadeshi* movement and bolster the "Made in India" brand, since a higher growth in the manufacturing sector would result in greater employment, increasing purchasing power and reducing the demand slump.

Swadeshi provides a solution to a stagnant manufacturing sector...

A severe lag in the manufacturing sector exacerbates India's despair. With the share of the manufacturing sector in GDP remaining sticky, hovering at around 18% for the past few years, revival of this sector remains a key challenge. Not only have key domestic industries like textile and clothing fallen behind in global markets, they are now finding it difficult to survive in the domestic market on account of fierce import competition. Despite its potential to harness abundant labour and natural resources, India relies extensively on imports. In order to accommodate this lag the Indian government has been promoting its "Made/Make in India" campaign, however the results seem to be largely dissatisfactory.

Several schemes such as ASPIRE (Scheme for Promotion of Innovation, Entrepreneurship and Agro-Industry), NMCP

(National Manufacturing Competitiveness Programme) and the ZED (Zero Defect and Zero Effect) have been designed to supplement this campaign, but such schemes aren't powerful enough to provide the immense push required to compensate for this enormous lag. Whilst there are sectors like auto components, steel and engineering companies in India which claim that they can compete well with China and Chinese companies, there also exist sectors like electronic manufacturing, wherein India is way behind China and smaller countries like Malaysia and Singapore. The "Made in India" campaign requires Indian companies to take initiative and gain global competitiveness, however the situation is daunted with several challenges.

Having underscored the importance of "Made in India", it is equally crucial to set a stage for "Make in India". By ensuring investment by foreign companies, India has much to gain in terms of technological know-how. However India is not lucrative enough for multiple foreign manufacturers. Around 60 Taiwanese companies have set up operations but not all of them have started manufacturing in India. In spite of the political disconnect with China, Taiwanese companies have cumulatively invested close to $200 billion over the years in China, which is significantly larger than that in India. Even American companies like SanDisk, a manufacturer of flash memory which outsources to China and Taiwan, does not want to manufacture in India. SanDisk president and COO Sanjay Mehrotra says: "Manufacturing in India means an investment of billions of dollars for us. It is an investment risk which we are not ready to take at the moment. The technology and infrastructure does not exist in India." Thus, India needs to strengthen its infrastructure which will be key to receiving investment from abroad as well as providing a strong base for India MSMEs.

Furthermore, Indian manufacturing is far from being "smart" as is the case in other emerging economies. The "Make in India" and "Made in India" initiatives, which lie at the core of our *Swadeshi* imperative, need to be coupled with an impetus on digitalization in order to be efficient and competitive. A major reason for our technological deficiency is the absence of proper development at the grassroots level. Thus, we require an intensive revival of *Swadeshi* which will help stir up manufacturing at the grassroots level as it did in the 1900s by strengthening the coir and cottage industries, and help overcome the structural deficiency which plagues the Indian manufacturing sector.

A united effort to dispel the unfortunate disparity betwixt genders...

The World Economic Forum's Global Gender Gap 2020 report shows how India slipped down from 108th to 112th on the Gender Gap Index (GGI) in 2019. This trend in the GGI which takes into account four primary aspects: Health, Education, Economy and Politics, is evidence of societal retrogression. India has consistently ranked low on the Gender Gap Index. Another measure of this divide can be seen in the sharp decline in female workers as a percentage of the total labour force.

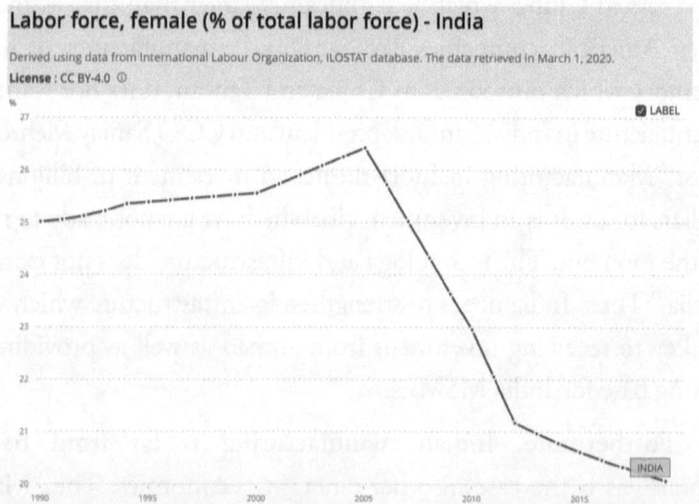

This relative disadvantage of women in India can be attributed to the difficulties present in the four aforementioned spheres. There exist several NGOs and governmental organizations aiming to better this situation, however progress has remained snail-like. This is primarily because little effort is made to tackle this power imbalance at the roots. Giving women the ability to support themselves economically is a major way out of this swamp and the path to this solution lies in a *Swadeshi* revival. Reducing our reliance on foreign goods and adopting the practice of purchasing and producing domestic goods could have unforeseen benefits to combat gender disparity in the country.

As imported goods are reduced, a vacuum is created within the market, encouraging start-ups to sprout in India from all sectors. As we enter a new decade, we have increased the emphasis on gender equality, which is reflective in the increased number of women-led businesses in India. In the light of the increased role of women in business, if a vacuum were to be created in the market, it would encourage Indian enterprises led by men and women to fill in the gaps. This does help achieve greater female representation in an urban industrial setting. Nevertheless, one must consider the fact that the situation in an urban setting is still relatively better than a rural setting. This is in itself another reason to revive *Swadeshi* for it will have a greater positive impact on the gender disparity in rural localities.

Several forms of labour work in multiple states of India are traditionally done by women such as Bengali embroidery and handicrafts from Bengal or the tea leaf pickers from Kerala. If co-operative businesses can be formed on the basis of the product and the geographical locations, one can initiate a successful business. Such was the case of AMUL, which is owned by three million farmers and has led to economic independence and empowerment of the women in Gujarat. As most dairy-related activities were primarily handled by women of the state, it led to greater gender equality in terms of financial status. Similarly, if women in a non-urban setting, who specialize in certain skills due to cultural influence can form co-operatives they will have a greater reach in the Indian market.

Cultural influence on specialization of skills can lead to the production of goods that are native to our country. This can be seen in one of India's oldest and most successful co-operative - Lijjat Papad. Manufacturing a variety of products from indigenous goods like *papads, roti* and *masala* to more common goods like liquid and powdered detergent. If women in traditional jobs form co-operatives and capitalize, during such an opportunity, it would strongly benefit the country economically. This may lead to the start of wide-spread culturally influenced co-operatives led by women thus reducing the gender gap economically.

A greater representation of women economically, throughout the country would cause a ripple effect, wherein empowered and successful women would inspire and advocate a new generation of women to have easy access to education. In the long term, this would improve the literacy rate and standard of living for the country, moreover educating increased number of women would serve as the foundation to overcome barriers that women face today. In short, our country will utilize the potential that has long remain suppressed.

The vitality of strong domestic manufacturing is reinforced by weakening global links. The *Swadeshi* imperative will be climacteric in bolstering resilience...

Since the dawn of the globalization, economic integration has become a norm. Manufacturing supply chains have become more convulsed than ever with every nation inevitably depending on another. If Japan for instance suffers a natural calamity, the ripples are felt globally in the form of semiconductor chip shortages. Integrated supply chains have indubitably reduced economic costs and nations all over have enjoyed its fruits. However, the difficulty with an over reliance on global supply chains was felt first during the 2008 financial meltdown, and the present coronavirus pandemic resonates the same. During the early days of the pandemic, inflation in India was expected to increase on account of supply shortages of electronic equipments which arrive as imports from China. This is but one commodity out of multiple others which India imports. With a global level lockdown, India will be unable to continue production in multiple sectors which rely on such imports. The intensity of this disruption is yet not felt in entirety, because India itself has halted domestic production on account of the ensuing lockdown.

As economies all across keep their borders shut, each country would scramble in need for goods which they have never manufactured. Similar would be the case with India. It is unrealistic for one to expect India to manufacture every product within its boundaries, however, greater production of goods like electronic products will help soften the blow. Furthermore, with the *Swadeshi* revival placing focus on the development of MSMEs (Micro, Small and Medium Enterprises) and production of other essentials such as textile, India will develop the resilience needed to insulate itself from external shocks.

As the COVID-19 pandemic escalates, the risks inherent in global supply chains are more apparent than ever and there exists a strong possibility of a Manufacturing Renaissance. Rather than awaiting a return to business as usual, with manufacturing activities concentrated in countries where labour is cheap and plentiful, advanced-economy companies are shifting their focus to the lowest-wage workers of all: robots. When uncertainty rises, global value chains suffer. Based on past data, one can predict that a 300% increase in uncertainty - as the COVID-19 pandemic seems likely to produce - would reduce global supply-chain activity by 35.4%.

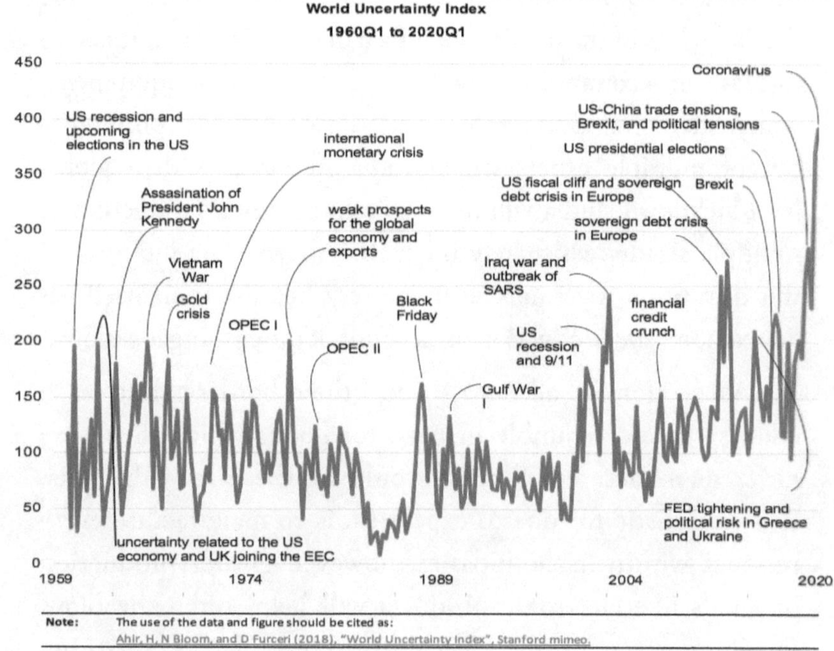

Note: The use of the data and figure should be cited as:
Ahir, H, N Bloom, and D Furceri (2018), "World Uncertainty Index", Stanford mimeo.

As a result firms no longer consider the cost savings of off-shoring to be worth the risk. At a time when adopting robots is cheaper than ever, the incentive to re-shore production is even stronger. The arithmetic is simple. A company in, say, the United States of America would have to pay an American worker a lot more than, say, a Vietnamese or Bangladeshi one. But a United States of America-based robot would not demand wages at all, let alone benefits like health insurance or sick leave. Investment in robots is not new. Advanced-economy firms have been pursuing it since the mid-1990s, led by the automotive industry, which can account for 50-60% of a country's robot stock. When the 2008 crisis struck, some countries, such as Germany, already had enough robots to minimize the importance of labour costs in production. Many others, aided by the sharp post-2008 decline in interest rates relative to wages, boosted robot adoption and re-shored a larger share of production. This trend poses a major threat to many developing countries' growth models, which depend on low-cost manufacturing and exports of intermediate inputs.

Australia's Telstra and Optus, and Britain's Virgin Media - all of which have offshore units in India and the Philippines - have announced plans to recruit hundreds of staff back home. Telstra, which heavily relies on its Philippine facility for customer service, initially said it would hire 1,000 temporary workers, but later raised that figure to 3,500. Optus sought to fill 500 vacancies saying that while the company had previously believed "its diversity of locations would make us resilient to any disruptions", this was no longer the case. But the bigger lasting change from the pandemic will likely involve the wider use of Artificial Intelligence to handle tasks currently performed by human beings. Telstra, for instance, which was already planning to slash customer service calls by two-thirds by 2022, now intends to accelerate its use of AI. CEO Andy Penn says, "(We) will be using this as an opportunity to further digitize and automate our business." The "on-shoring" of jobs and the increased use of AI will have a big impact on countries that for years have benefitted from taking on the back-office operations of multinationals. India, in particular, was a trailblazer. As of 2017, the industry employed nearly four million Indians and raked in revenues of more than $150 billion, according to trade body NASSCOM. India is evidently heavily reliant on providing services outsourced by foreign companies, but this model of development is clearly under threat. A *Swadeshi* revival is a prospective substitute employment and growth source once the outsourcing industry loses its charm.

In Central and Eastern Europe, some countries have responded to this challenge by investing in robots themselves. However the path for India in the wake of this Renaissance is a major conundrum. First, India does not have the manufacturing base to invest in robotics, and second, it cannot afford to transition at the expense of labour employment. Even though a transition would be beneficial in the long run (Schumpeterian Creative Destruction), one cannot race into it. A simple solution to this conundrum lies yet again in a *Swadeshi* revival which would help develop manufacturing at a grass root level, and shall overtime not only expand wealth but also, via education (as a consequence of economic upliftment) help convert a pool of largely unskilled labour into an educated workforce. Greater wealth and an educated workforce shall enable a smooth transition into a robotic age. This does not however imply that the *Swadeshi* revival remain devoid of a robotic touch. We need to ensure that this *Swadeshi* revival remains modern; one which enables artificial intelligence to augment human labour. This is of critical importance for India to cover up its lag in the field of technology. An expanding domestic manufacturing sector would most certainly serve to reduce the extent of this over reliance.

Revisiting a sector which India boldly skipped in the past...

Exports of goods is a major segment where India lags. A major reason for the same is the fact that India transitioned from an agricultural economy directly to a tertiary one, not having gone through the manufacturing (secondary) phase. As a consequence a majority of the workforce remains unskilled and inequality seems to be widening. Experts have cited examples like the UK and China wherein a manufacturing phase in the development model enabled theses countries to uplift majority of the workforce economically, hence strengthening education and skill. As for India, the rural population, which makes up a majority of the total populace, are trapped in a vicious cycle of poverty and illiteracy. The *Swadeshi* revival, via development at the grassroots level, can help break this vicious cycle and enable an expansion of our export industry, which is extremely weak when compared to economies of similar size. Expanding the domestic manufacturing base is bound to help increase exports, however India should not follow an export-led growth model; since over reliance on exports is bound to backfire when global markets panic, as is the case today.

India boasts of a young population, however having a young populace does not amount to a demographic dividend. If the country is unable to absorb its youth productively via employment, this so called dividend may turn into a curse, with an excessive burden on the government's coffers in the form of unemployment benefits and schemes. Our nation has to focus on an internal growth model, and not an external one. If we succeed in raising the purchasing power of our rural populace, the demand growth will erase the existing slump. This would further augment consumer confidence and the economic machinery shall be functioning effectively again. The means to such an end lies yet again in grassroots development for which our *Swadeshi* initiative is fundamental.

As mentioned above, a majority of India's population thrives in the rural sector, which accounted for almost 75% of the total population as of 2018.

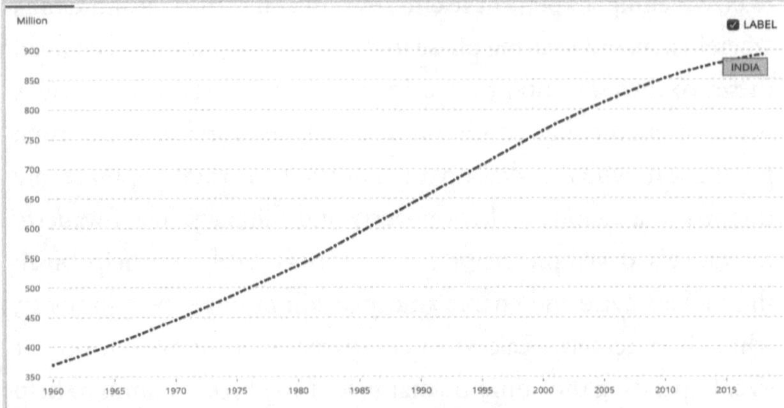

Strengthening the Make in India Movement, would allow the development of the entire rural sector through the encouragement of manufacturing goods and services. This would enable indigenous regional goods to become more widely available across the country, allowing the country to lean more towards self-sufficiency. Even though this goes against the core beliefs of globalization, this step is vital for reviving the economy from its slowdown.

A *Swadeshi* revival is no panacea. Our nation will have to navigate through complexities in order to ensure its success...

As we advance its importance, it is vital to recognize that a revival of *Swadeshi* today is not devoid of complexity. There are several stumbling blocks that the nation will have to carefully circumvent in order to make this dream a reality. First, a huge fiscal stimulus is required to ramp up infrastructure and domestic manufacturing. The problem with the same is the addition to an enormous debt which already exists. However during a structural downturn, one where private investment remains dampened, the onus is on the government to shell out the money. India will have to risk increasing debt in order to implement a broad scale *Swadeshi* revival. However, excessive debt and overshooting fiscal deficit numbers do not augur well for any economy, and thus, the solution lies in extensive public-private partnerships.

A related challenge to this solution is the fraught relationship between the state and the private sector. In India neither the state nor the private sector commands great legitimacy. This problem has a long history, but have been intensified after the government corruption scandals of the 2000s and the lending practices of the past decade. Given this experience, bureaucrats will be reluctant to sign off on public sector projects, while the anxious private sector will continue to lack appetite for ambitious projects that demand long-term commitment. None of this should be taken as a counsel of despair. For the government to pull the economy out of a slowdown two ingredients are essential: recognizing the true extent and nature of the problem and instituting reliable data systems for good policy navigation. Otherwise, not just Indian policymakers, but their Washington advisers too, risk remaining in the dark.

Another major problem associated with the advancement of *Swadeshi* would be the execution of a certain amount of protectionism. A major reason that imports flood Indian markets is primarily due to the fact that foreign manufacturers produce better quality of goods at a lower cost. In other words, India is not as efficient as other countries are at manufacturing. Thus, in order for domestic manufacturing to develop to globally competitive levels, India will have to adopt protectionist measures such as import tariffs or production subsidies to domestic industries. In doing so India is sure to face great criticism on the global platform. In this regard, the government will have to strike a delicate balance between global connection and isolationism.

Over the years we have seen that whilst global connection has its advantages, it also suffers a major disadvantage since a local problem becomes global. It is important to understand that it is not just India, which seeks to develop a certain amount of economic independence. Countries all over the world are re-shoring production and strengthening their self-sustaining capabilities. Several industries have been demanding additional doses of protection for a number of years, but it is only in the recent past that the government has begun responding to their demands. A major challenge to Indian diplomacy would be to highlight and use the *Swadeshi* revival as a tool to advance our soft-power and prevent it from being labelled as means to protectionism.

In his 2018-19 budget speech, Arun Jaitley had announced his decision to make "a calibrated departure" from the past policy by increasing customs duties on mobile phones and some electronic components as a measure to strengthen electronic manufacturing. The reason, to incentivize domestic value addition and to further the objectives of Make in India. Nirmala Sitharaman has adopted the same policy of increasing customs duties to protect the interests of domestic players engaged in the production of cashew kernels, PVC, auto parts, synthetic rubbers and a range of electronic products, among others. However, it needs to be pointed out that the government's policy of import protection can provide only temporary relief to the industries; "domestic value addition" can be effectively incentivized by providing necessary conditions for the expansion of micro, small and medium enterprises (MSMEs). MSMEs can well act as the magic bullet, for this sector can help expand both manufacturing capacities and job creation.

The irony is that despite understanding the value of MSMEs, successive governments have fallen short of meeting the critical needs of these enterprises, especially, availability of credit on favourable terms. India urgently needs development of financial institutions geared to meeting the critical needs of MSMEs, which exist in several developed and emerging economies. This is another major obstacle to the success of our *Swadeshi* revival. Our financial system is weak on account of rising Non-Profitable Assets (NPAs) and an improper balance between excessive and limited regulation.

The IL&FS crash on 2018, was the beginning of a prolonged credit crunch in our financial sector. Following bank scams and scandals have only worsened this situation. While the RBI is making efforts to lower lending rates by diffusion of liquidity, banks have been reluctant in passing this relief to borrowers. Economists state that the high number of NPAs in the banking and non-banking financial sector are a consequence of the 2016 demonetization worsened by structural issues. The government has to ensure the existence of robust financing if it is to incentivize private investment, which is crucial to ensuring the success of the *Swadeshi* agenda. A piece of evidence that could serve as a solution to the conundrum of developing the financing model for revival of manufacturing is that in all successful countries, private investment has followed public investment. The government should perhaps carry out a course correction by going back to a public investment-led financing model for development. This will in turn trigger the revival of investor sentiments in general, which has been at unacceptably low levels in the past few years.

Alone we can do so little, together we can do so much. An appeal to all Indians to help rebuild our motherland...

Mahatma Gandhi once said, "My nationalism is as broad as my *Swadeshi*, I want India's rise so that the whole world may benefit." A sense of unity and belonging is as vital as charting a plan. For *Swadeshi* to benefit our country, every Indian needs to take responsibility. Manufacturing and production are futile in the absence of demand, thus we should try and make use of products made in India as our little support towards making this dream come true. Just like the *Swadeshi* movement of 1905 united Indians towards strengthening their motherland, the revival today requires no less. The time is ripe for India to embrace its immense potential and ensure a sustainable future.

Section

3

FOLLOWING THE FOOTSTEPS OF ARGUMENTATIVE INDIANS

This section is a collection of works on abstract yet contemporary discourses. Each topic is a typical mix of economic, political and social sciences. Studying each topic in the absence of bias, an effort is made to account for every possible facet. Wherever an existing idea is used, credit has been given to the respective intellect. This section is a tribute to all those intellects who dare to scrutinize and criticize widely accepted notions in the face of pushback, be it from society to the government. Each piece has been inspired by the works of academics such as Amartya Sen, Shashi Tharoor and Ramachandra Guha, whose contributions have been vital to the spirit of argumentation.

1. **Economic 'BRANDING'**
2. **'Convergence' - Myth or Reality**
3. **Debating Democracy**
4. **Anonymity on the Internet: Shield or Weapon**
5. **Climate Change - Sparking the World's Largest Refugee Crisis**

1

Economic "BRANDING"

A nation's global influence is more than the sum of its growth, development and military figures. The additional piece to this puzzle is what I would like to call "the Economic Brand" of every nation; an aspect which may not be of direct assistance, but can prove to be supportive at critical junctures.

This piece was completed on the 29th of July, 2019.

In his research paper *"The Role of Brands in Human Culture"*, Philip Kotler notes that, "…An increasing number of companies see their brand as the platform for running their businesses. The brand creates an identity for the product and/or company in the marketplace. It requires the company to think deeply about its mission, vision and values. The company has to work hard at developing the image that it wants customers to have of the offering. The brand must not only convince prospective customers and draw them to the brand, but also be deeply believed in by the employees and other stakeholders of the company…" This note about belief is critical, for branding is a psychological entity that manifests economic values in firms of all sizes. (Philip Kotler is widely regarded as the most influential marketer of all times.)

Similarly, every nation has, what I would like to call, an "Economic Brand" which corresponds to aspects mentioned above by Philip, however on a broader and more macro level, yet in the end resulting in "belief", "loyalty" and "value", all of which would be as critical to any economy as it would be to an enterprise. Every country has soft power; a source of global influence coinciding with and culminating into an "image". This image in turn mirrors the "Economic Brand" of a nation. This seemingly benign facet can be an immensely influencing prospect, prima facie, given its role in developing investor confidence. This "confidence" is no absolute measure with set parameters to evaluate, but remains largely subjective and hence premised on perception.

This aspect is quite often the reason why an economy which though relatively worse off, as per standard economic indicators, and hence consequently likely to fail would not, whereas other nations performing equally poorly or even a tad bit better may astonishingly collapse. In other words, it is the nation upholding a stronger and broader image that would prevail.

This image is a culminating product of experience and performance of countries, which add on to their respective credibilities. A few nations like the USA have strong credibility and hence strong "soft power", given their history as striving democratic institutions. The USA since the 1700s has been transitioning towards stronger democratic constructs, whilst also promoting the same elsewhere. The Marshall Aid, an assistance to help nations restructure themselves from the spoils of the World War, is a major factor accounting for the extensive soft power the USA has today.

Thus, it follows that past and present political institutions are major determinants of the "Brand Value" of any nation. Consequently, it also follows that nations like North Korea or Mexico, unlike the USA, would not relish the emoluments of a "good image", for they have been and still are drenched in ghastly Extractive Political Institutions.

Extractive Political Institutions are political regimes wherein decisions are taken by, and for, a narrow group of people (elites). Centralization of power is yet another parameter to measure the degree of the same, with greater centralization of power reducing chaos within an Extractive Political Institution. This in turn results in Extractive Economic Institutions, which concentrate economic gains in the hands of these same few, further facilitating the formation of Extractive Political Institutions. It is indeed a vicious cycle.

Daron Acemoglu and James A. Robinson talk of this spiralling relation between Extractive Political Institutions and Extractive Economic Institutions in their brilliant book "*Why*

Nations Fail". In a nutshell this spiral essentially looks at a bilateral causal relation between the two and thus evading an Extractive Economic Institution (which is inherently bound to shatter the economy) would require **"Inclusive"** Political Institutions and vice versa. Nations that have been successful in breaking out of this cycle have developed a good image with South Korea being an exemplary of the same, having relatively recently become more democratic.

However it would not hold true if one says that a good image accrues to only those nations boasting of inclusive institutions. There do exist nations like China; a communist regime and hence inherently devoid of an Inclusive Political Institution, yet having a strong image. The answer to this quandary would lie in further broadening of the reasons leading to a good image, out of which one shall gain international economic status, which is inclusive of achievements and importance. China today is a major world exporter, which it remains given its lower prices and progressing quality. However it is equally important to make note of the fact that China, though en route to becoming the next global superpower when judged on economic importance and geo-strategic influence, would perhaps not gain such a status, given its relatively weaker image (hence softer "soft power"!). The presence of a relatively less prominent image can be attributed to, as mentioned earlier, the absence of Inclusive Political Institutions. Thus, as evident these few "causes" in isolation aren't explanatory and shall lie defunct in the face of any situation. A proper reasoning behind the causes of the "Economic Brand" can be formulated only when looked at as being a flux of both politics and economics fused via a social outlook.

Time as a factor behind the strengthening of this image isn't straightforward either. We have the nations like the USA having built such an image over centuries whereas economies like China have done so (if not surpassing the former, then certainly reaching almost at par) over a span of just a few decades. Whilst the long span of time is an indication of stability and solidity, China's short miraculous growth is emblematic of agility, progress and innovation.

Having established how one's "Brand" exists in relation with time, history, polity and the economy, it is rudimentary to recognize the importance of the same using an interesting model, which posed an enigma to me, when I first thought of the same.

The USA has a debt of over 100% of its GDP as of 2018, and yet remains a global superpower. Analogously, Japan too has a massive debt of over 200% of its GDP and yet remains a thriving developed economy (even though both these countries are facing a few constraints as of today).

Greece on the other hand suffered and caused much despair to the entire Euro-Zone following its crisis in 2009, which was a result of a "panic of default" as its debt reached a mere 15.4% of its GDP. It is indeed astonishing to witness Greece, with a much lower proportionate debt to GDP than the USA and Japan, collapsing whilst the other two have not and do not face much risk of collapsing even today.

The answer to the above conundrum as projected by many is the "brand" as we have discussed throughout. Yet this answer, of the reasoning behind this conundrum, being "the image" or "the brand" is too simplistic. In the words of Shashi Tharoor "it would form an easy argument, but not a good argument". Forming a good argument would require an analysis of the differences between these economies that shout out the reasons behind the corresponding difference in their "images".

A striking difference betwixt the debt in Japan and that in Greece is that the former is largely held domestically, unlike the latter which was gravely dependent on foreign investors and hence foreign debt. This difference would in itself, perhaps, stamp this comparison as flawed, since we would be dealing with two entirely different scenarios with different debt patterns, yet this is not the case for Japan is not devoid of foreign debt entirely. In fact foreign debt in absolute amounts was still larger in Japan than that held in Greece, even though internally the proportion of domestic debt as a percentage of the total debt is larger in Japan.

Now Japan having major portions of domestic debt suffers minimal risk because, domestic debt in itself suffers minimal risk; for citizens would not have their own economy collapse, as no person would wish for one's own downfall. Hence given the relative stability of domestic debt, it creates a perception of solidarity as well as consistency; this in concurrence with the Japanese model and history of a miraculous growth, and adds great credibility on an international platform. Furthermore Japan shows minimal signs of defaulting on the domestic debt.

Greece on the other hand, post the entrance into the Euro-Zone confessed in 2004 to having lied about its debt in order to get around the Maastricht Criteria. The governments that came to power time and again complained of their predecessors having left a debt larger than that portrayed. Promising a reduction of the debt they ended up doing exactly what their predecessors had done, only to be revealed when a new party came to power. In the eyes of any investor, naive or experienced, this would reflect a worrisome picture given the absence of discipline and trust in their existing political construct. The "Ease of Doing Business Scores" by the world bank for 2007 reflect quite well

Japan's prominence over Greece (the scores are available at: http://www.doingbusiness.org/en/reports/global-reports/doing-business-2007). All such factors which portray the existence of weak political and economic institutions account for the poor "brand" or "image" of Greece. It was this poor image which facilitated its crisis via a "panic of default" as its debt touched just 15.4% of GDP. Had Greece had a stronger/better "image" it would have perhaps had more time to restructure itself in a way so as to prevent a crisis.

Comparison between the USA and Greece would also indicate similar outcomes when based on similar parameters. As evident from the collation above, healthy economic and political institutions result in a good "image" which in turn reinforces that (healthy economic and political institutions) which strengthens it in the first place. This cycle, where more prominent, has quite clearly an edge over the others with greater inflows being just one advantage amongst several. This does in a way explain why nations diverge or converge, and as to why nations fail or prosper. This discussion is greatly in tandem with Acemoglu and Robinson's study of the same in their book *"Why Nations Fail"*.

In a world where Trump's protectionism is gaining prominence and perceptions are turning against free trade, people tend to remain oblivious to the importance of an "image" and "soft power" which may not be of direct assistance, but can prove to be supportive in critical junctures, wherein prospects of nations moving on parallel lines would be judged. Such an "image" has been and will be of great importance and should not suffer neglect.

2

Convergence - Myth or Reality?

With advancing technology, we tend to believe that humanity as a whole is moving forward. Scholars often assert the idea of nations reaching equal status with time. However this "Convergence" that people talk about may not quite be as true as one expects.

Thomas Friedman talks of the modern world being en route to becoming a "flatter" one. It seems only logical to envisage the globe, which today remains largely premised on free-market dictums, to establish equal standards of political, social and economic existence. The ensuing trade-wars and a rise in protectionism do propose a stance hostile to globalization and liberalization, yet this stance in itself seems unlikely to obviate modern classical ideologies and markets.

The technological boom and innovation have over time facilitated smooth flow of resources and knowledge across borders, effectively narrowing communication and transfer barriers; barriers which were anathemas for civilizations like the Aztecs, who in isolation, remained oblivious to the revolutionary developments in the "fertile crescent"; developments which would with time be a primary force behind the ascent of Europeans to global hegemony amidst the unfortunate others. Jarred Diamond talks of the same in his book *"Guns, Germs and Steel"*, whilst presenting his geographical hypothesis as a reasoning behind the divergence amongst nations. Though heavily scrutinized as being an incomplete argument, it is worth a read, not to perhaps straitjacket yourself to his views, but to develop a broader and better picture of historical developments. Jarred explains how the Spanish conquistadors were in convenient geographical proximity to the Middle-East and hence had access to steel weaponry and gunpowder. Such developments would be god-like powers for the technically inferior Aztec and Incas of the Americas, and were a primary motif behind their downfall.

Daron Acamoglu and Robinson, discuss in their book *"Why Nations Fail"*, the divergence at great length; impressive, given a wonderful balance between dogma and examples, with the latter justifying brilliantly the former. In reading their book, one can effectively trace the trends in global inequality over centuries; inequality within nations and amongst them too. Delving into the past, one finds it difficult to thread a general well-defined relational movement of one nation's prosperity relative to other nations. In the past, the fall and rise of civilizations as well as their corresponding periods of largesse were largely products of endogenous factors, for there were no tools to accommodate exogenous contributions; the tools in question being ones which facilitate globalization via a free flow of commodities, knowledge and ideologies. Our hyper-globalized world today relishes gains from a removal of such barriers.

Inventions and discoveries are organic to human reasoning and ingenuity, having taken place throughout the course of history. However, inventions seldom discovered ways to proliferate over regions thus disabling most from relishing ensuing gains. This non-transferability was partly due to an absence of the very means to facilitate the same (transportation and technology), and partly due to political thoughts and institutions prevailing in certain societies. The Roman Empire is known to have disabled several innovators from advancing the state, for the "ruling elite" saw innovation led to "creative destruction" and the ensuing circulation of elites as a precarious threat to their dominance. Global history bears testimony to the repetitive downsizing of innovation, yet when innovative developments did take place, nations and regions often shifted further up the ladder of global hegemony. An interesting trait of such movements is the supervening hegemony which arises, for when the new "innovating elites" and their nations gain ground, there inevitably results an increasing inequality between the nation in question and other nations. Thus it follows that innovative developments in the past actually furthered divergence, for they concentrated the opulence in specific regions due to a lack of transferability. The divergence between the Europeans and the native Americans is exemplary of the same.

Convergence is said have gained prominence following technological developments which effectively lowered barriers between nations. However the same is barely true in the absence of economic and political ideals which uphold the principle of "united-development" of all instead of "self-development"; which in turn demands democracy as a prerequisite for the such ideals. Now the natural barriers, like an expansive ocean or an arid desert betwixt regions diminishing any incentive to embark trade venture weren't impediments once ships were constructed and trade routes developed. Then inter-continental trade gained ground, yet the same in no way led to Convergence, for such trade expeditions were fuelled by mercantilist motives; mercantilists were major proponents behind colonialism, which dictated the rise of oneself, premised on the sufferance of another.

Then when did Convergence begin?

Most look at the Industrial Revolution in England as the answer. Railways were setup and innovation-led-capital-formation shot up productivity, slowly producing chic suburbs which were once dusty forlorn mofussils. This enhanced the efficacy of the new born converging trend unlike in the past also because England was democratic by justifiable standards with similar developments taking place in the Americas. This proliferated the essence of free-trade and globalization, both premised on mutual gains and not "economic involution".

"This would enable all to progress and develop." - OR WOULD IT?

If the kernel of - "this would enable all to progress and develop" - logical flow was so simplistic with such a satisfactory end, the need for economists would indeed diminish! Evidently, the current scenario draws a narrative reflective of a world, governed by dictums similar or more progressive (by free-market standards) than those during the initiation of Convergence, facing what I would like to call a "Diverging Convergence" (essentially a diminishing convergence). The possible reasons shall be discussed presently.

For starters, even the Industrial Revolution which paved the way for human advancement both technologically and ideologically, sowing the seeds for a technological revolution, ironically, at the time of its initiation widened the already exiting divergence. Western and Eastern Europe witnessed diverging trends since the "Black Death" or the "Bubonic Plague", which the paved way for greater inclusivity in Western European regions, but a second serfdom (and hence greater inequality, suppression and oppression) in the East. Building on such existing institutional difference, the Industrial Revolution served as a critical juncture, which would propel England to heights of Global Hegemony whilst leaving the Eastern European nations dawdling. Only much later would these nations make efforts to reduce the lag.

With ground breaking technological developments in the recent centuries we have witnessed what economists like to call the "hockey stick of growth"; showing how nations have in terms of the GDP excelled massively in recent years such that in comparison to the long past, a plot of GDP with time looks much like a hockey stick.

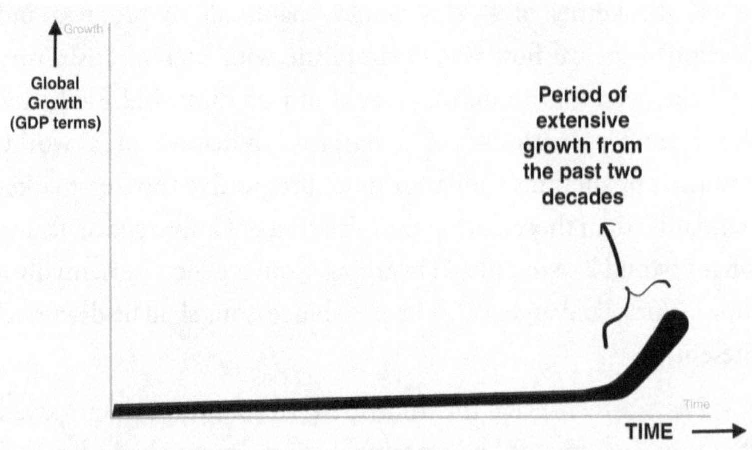

With such exponential progress and growth, nations have advanced immensely. One would naturally expect that grave inequality reminiscent of the past, would today remain absent. However the scenario prevalent remains direly incongruent to such expectations. In fact, current growth and development seem to have run out of steam, for inequality seems to be on the rise; almost as though the factors which initially led to a Convergence are today working in reverse thrust, furthering divergence in lieu of convergence.

There do exist emerging economies and there always shall. However of these nations, a limited few sustain long period growth, which remains quintessential to attain at par status with global hegemons. A research conducted by Ruchir Sharma illustrates "that only one-third of emerging markets have been able to grow at an annual rate of 5% or more. Less the one-fourth have kept that pace for two decades, and one-tenth for three decades. Just four countries have maintained this rate of growth for four decades and two (South Korea and Taiwan) have done so five decades." In other words the "morality-rate" of such countries is as high as that of stocks.

In the absence of sustained economic growth nations fail to attain equal status. A failure in growth consistency and sustenance arises primarily in response to the "middle income" trap; which states that countries emerge primarily by replicating the growth process of developed economies, in essence following the Lewis Model of growth, however suffer stagnation once gains from mere reallocation of resources exhaust; an absence of innovation compounds this predicament, hence lowering the odds of sustained growth. Why would such economies fail to innovate? The answer is the "Dutch Disease" - When nations follow the export-led growth model, they are reliant on specific sectors in which they trade and hence neglect other sectors that could be innovation stimulating. Often emerging economies receive prominence with the discovery of natural resources, which in turn results in the "Natural Resource Curse" as they get increasingly ignorant of all sectors apart from energy, e.g., Middle East, Russia, Angola and the list carries on.

Quite interestingly so, being headlined as a prospective "global power" can be more often than not a double-edged sword; on the one hand capital inflows rise in response to rising investor confidence, yet on the other hand with an appreciating currency, the economy suffers in the export market; furthermore most of emerging economies have followed export-led growth models, having immense resource endowments [a excess in labour allows cheap manufacturing (China) or an extensive natural resource presence results in export of the same (Russia)].

The "Dutch Disease", as mentioned earlier is anathema to emerging markets, as their export-led growth model raises dependence on Western developed markets; thus a fall in demand due to fall in growth in the West would essentially indicate a fall in growth of the emerging market in question. This draws a picture of a vicious dependence which states that the growth of 'Emerging Market' remains premised on the Growth in the West, which in turn increases vulnerability.

The "Economics" of any nation/market remain unexplainable in the absence of due deference given to prevailing political constructs. Faulty leadership can often take a nation from Hunky Dory to Humpty Dumpty, examples of which aren't all that difficult to find; Russia for one under the extractive leadership of Putin and hence subject to his ideologies, and decisions has been subject to sanctions and alerts, which undermine its image and hinder its growth; Angola, yet another resource rich region, remains mired in poverty for its "ruler" is fraudulent and grafting; The possible India saga as a global power is threatened immensely by a crony political construct.

Paul Krugman justifiably labels the current global scenario as "Depression Economics". Developed nations over the world suffer dampened demand and hence stagnating growth. The USA is exemplary of the same; Apple recently lowered its revenue outlook, which seems fitting given the mentioned conditionality. China as per a recent study by the UNCTAD titled *"The Trade Delusion"*, however remains one nation out of a few, displaying increasing productivity and efficiency. Yet analysts expect China to witness lower growth in the near future, given the trade wars and tensions, and its emerging middle class, which in turn extinguishes its major Herculean leverage - cheap labour. However there do exist economies like India that hold immense potential.

Yet an interesting question would be whether **"Stagnating developed economies"** would make it easier for emerging economies to catch up and hence facilitate convergence? It remains highly unlikely that such a model should be idealized even though it may ease convergence, because: First as mentioned earlier, stagnating Western developed nations can be inimical to the development of the emerging markets, with the latter remaining heavily dependent on the former; Second even if the pattern does roll out the way contested in the question, such a convergence would in fact be regressive, for it would ultimately lead either to:

1. Divergence if emerging markets surpass **"Stagnating developed economies"** or

2. Even if they stay at par, all would suffer stagnation.

Many have attributed this cataclysmic occurrence to neo-liberal capitalism, which manifests in innumerable economies, if not all.

It is indubitably true that the neo-liberal mindset which dictates large many markets today is inimical to equality, yet this equality is one persisting between people and not nations.

For ages people have associated Convergence between nations with corresponding reductions in inequality between citizens, and it is only logical to presume so, because any developing economy would essentially have its benefits shared by its residents. Yet the same is barely true in the current scenario. My stance should not be confused as one being anti-trade or anti-capitalist. My stance is one against excessive deregulation, against cronyism and against the ensuing oligarchy/monopoly that emerge. When I mention the presence of increasing inequality, the reasoning behind the same is that almost all gains from trade (globalization) are taken by a few rich and the rest remain mainly stagnated. Such an absence of proportionate sharing could arise out of Pikkety's theory of a "skill-biased technical change"; compounded with persisting cronyism, exacerbates deregulation and hence rising Ponzi schemes and excessively risky financial ventures, which together formed the 2008 financial crisis - an economic tragedy. The incredulously large incomes of hedge fund managers and bankers, defy Friedman's claim of the absence of a "free lunch". This "free lunch" that such profiteers enjoy isn't all that free, but is composed of the others "lunches", ipso facto implicative of a loss of a majority, premised on the gains of a few. These are but a few hazards of the current deregulated (a striking trait of neo-liberal capitalism) scenario.

China an ideologically "communist" regime today remains mired in inequality, which is a presence one would least expect in a communist nation. All developed and emerging markets today face similar handicaps; India mired in cronyism; Russia remains stagnated; the Middle East still in disrepair, subject to extractive political and economic institutions; the USA suffers similar malfeasances; Britain subject to the slow-growth dilemma and the productivity puzzle; the list remains unending. Such stagnation and slow growth often demand fiscal stimuli for a kick-start. Paul Krugman advocates the need for demand side measures to evade such "depression economics". Though deficits are opposed by many, it seems like the "Keynsian Compact", which had found prominence in the 1930s, requires recapitulation.

Today we remain confronted with a scenario wherein Convergence seems to have fossilized as an element of the past. We need to give impetus to the same. Divergence prowls our lives; divergence between nations and people. Even to a naif (naive) observer like myself it seems that a world totally Converged, id est (i.e., that is) a "Flat World", seems highly improbable. Yes, I do acknowledge that over centuries of advancement and refinement both in terms of thought and action, we as a world have become more informed, connected and affable. We all do have access to the platform of hegemony, yet this platform remains and perhaps always will, small for all of the world. Hence it should follow that total inter-nation equality or "Absolute Convergence" remains a myth. Nations fall whilst others rise to prominence.

Argentina, once an opulent market, having a doubly effluent economy as Japan in not less than century, stagnated only to remain one-fourth of Japanese standards as of today. There, do and will, exist emerging markets out of which a few often collapse midway (the Arab Spring countries are exemplary of the same), whereas developed nations tend to stagnate. It seems as though there exists a cyclical flow organic to the global economic machinery; one which requires a constant replacement of existing hegemons by emerging nations, resulting from an ever-persistent "creative destruction". Anxiety and tension in the USA remain reflective in their actions and policy statements as China surfaces as a new superpower.

Myanmar and Vietnam pose as prospective markets and are potential paragons to the world, given they tread a path that professes an inclusive and righteous path. India holds promise no less than Vietnam and Myanmar, given its "rulers" keep the interests of the nation above their own. The Indian Constitution like every other remains indispensable and consequential, yet rough hewn political hacks make the same superfluous and weak. Almost every revolution finds its roots in infighting; infighting occurs when the residents raise their voices in dissent fulfilling their electoral obligations. We the plebeians are quintessential for reform and the onus of change rests on our shoulders. We shall continue our strife for equality; equality between humans and not one between nations, for total national Convergence/ Equality is resonant of a myth.

3

Debating Democracy

With democracies all over the world witnessing protests and discontent, scholars have started tasing questions on the viability of a democracy as a system. China, which has indeed grown exponential over the last few decades, has done so in the absence of a democratic setup. Many democracies, including India, seem to have been caught up in the throes of widespread discontent and despair. I, for one however, believe in the institution of a democracy and this piece is a defence of the same.

This piece was completed on the 12ᵗʰ of July, 2019.

As the world advances into an ever-progressing dynamic era of information technology, we seem confronted with an enigma; a perplexing rise in the number of protests as the world boasts its transition into a freer, safer and fairer world with the onset of a democratic spread over the past century. Unravelling this enigma is no herculean task for the claims of freedom, safety and justice are made in dire ignorance of a majority of the human populace living in the absence if these glossy virtues.

Democracies in praxis seem to exist in dire contrast and conflict from their dogmatic/theoretical selves. This is not to say that a democracy as a political institution is futile having run its course. Quite to the contrary, I believe that the nuclear thought behind democracy, one of equality and freedom, is sacrosanct and can exist only in a democracy. The justification for this belief lies in the deficiencies within alternative modes of governance. The alternatives, be it a dictatorship, a monarchy or meritocracy, all have a fatal flaw; they suppress expression and dissent, which is in turn crucial for them to maintain their primal advantage, STABILITY. Yet in course of maintaining stability, they not only suppress dissent but also innovation. History is evidence that several authoritarians in the past have worked to suppress innovation, in course to prevent yet another person of power (via wealth) from sprouting up.

Instances aren't hard to find, Kongo for centuries did not have a plough for their ruler feared the rise of landlords as a consequence of better production and hence better profitability. Rome is yet another example of the same wherein several innovations were quashed in fear of instability. This phenomena is explained quite interestingly in the book "*Why Nations Fail*" by Daron Acemoglu and James A. Robinson. However this suppression of expression (be it in the form innovation or dissent) over a period of time acts in opposition to its intended cause, because frustration when bottled in any community or society will find a way out sooner or later and can be revolutionary. Such uprisings may or not have the desired result; however one should not gauge its success only in terms of the immediate result, because often several protests are simply components of a larger, more impactful evolutionary process shaping the future.

For instance, it would be foolish to claim that the First Indian Independence Movement of 1857 was futile because independence was earned a century later due to an unrelated non-violence movement in 1947. There are three fundamental reasons to justify the foibles in the previous statement; first, every protest prior to the independence movement, big or small, served as a precedent to future protests, showing that people are dissatisfied and that people can and should protest; second, it helped spread the word and gain greater participation; third, it stirred a strong sense of nationalism as people of different cultures and creeds marched in unison to attain freedom from oppression.

"Is the democratic system of governance a failure?" - a question which finds itself in the midst of a multitude of academic discussions today. I believe that the democratic construct as a system of governance is not a failure. It is in fact the Snollygosters and charlatans masquerading as leaders that have stained democracy with a shade of failure. It is the many rough-hewn political hacks without an iota of loyalty or allegiance that have cast a shadow of defeat over democracy.

Yet the argument above points to yet another question - "If a democracy is not a failure, then how come such fraudsters rise to prominence in its political hierarchy; is it therefore a systemic issue?". This question is of great significance, for its answer highlights two major traits of any democracy - it is flawed and it is an evolving structure.

Why flawed? - Because for an ideal democracy to exist, the pillars supporting it (1. checks and balances, 2. rule of law and 3. democratic accountability, to name a few) need to be sturdy and in place. More often than not these pillars are either crumbling or sadly absent, leading to a democratic presence which works in contradiction to its virtues. This is precisely why, the Democracy Index Rankings published by *"The Economist"* places only 20 countries as functioning democracies, followed by several flawed democracies and hybrid regimes along with Russia (a democracy on paper) being labelled an authoritarian regime.

Why an evolving structure? - Because, the dearth of the crucial democratic pillars is not indicative of an implausibility of a democratic construct, but is indicative of friction and perhaps instability in the form of protest as well as dissent; friction which shall overhaul institutions and result in better democratic constructs. Centuries of instability have today resulted in a world much better than the past; not to say that our world is not plagued by hunger, economic inequality and injustice, however the absence of monarchies/authoritarians today have made the freedom of expression a whole lot more easier than it was. Millions of lives are unlikely to be lost on the commands of a few charlatans in our world, which remains more integrated and aware than ever before; thanks to the IT (information technology) wave, which in itself has a crucial role to play in shaping democracies.

Let's turn to India as an example, a democracy reaching its 70s, has indeed evolved into a better nation. The Indian state today is far from perfect; in fact it remains convulsed in poverty and underdevelopment, however it has come a long way from a "nation of fakirs and snake charmers to one with computer wizards and IT gurus". Our one party dynastic political system has evolved into a multi-party democracy. The caste system and patriarchal setup are diminishing in impact. The elections are most certainly not free and fair, with the apocryphal 2019 election results, however the presence of a political opposition along with an increasingly literate population (yet another dynamic of an evolving democratic structure) have the freedom to express their opinions. The Modi regime in India according to many is like Indira Gandhi's, one where chauvinism wins over rationalism. This is indeed troublesome, however as our population becomes more literate, reason will slowly take over and the power of juicy yet empty rhetoric/promises shall diminish. In short evolution shall take place as our pillars strengthen. The time for the completion of such an 'evolution', I suppose, shall remain an answer that only the future can provide.

Many would disagree with India as an archetypical democracy, and quite rightly so. Prime Minister Modi's rise to prominence despite the massive 2019 general strike and averse public sentiments, perhaps does indicate, in one way or another, an increasing tilt towards a system which is anything but a democracy. Which takes one to yet another perplexing situation: **Is it therefore possible for a democratic leader to convert a democracy into a despotic regime?**

The answer to this would lie in the weakness of democratic pillars. But this answer is in no way satisfactory.

To further discuss, let's look at a counterfactual reality, wherein India was an authoritarian regime, much like North Korea. In such a reality, the rise of Hindutva fundamentalism would most certainly witness its peak and several sectarian charlatans would witness a peak in power. This toxic combination along with a slew of irrational sycophants would result in a relentless pursuit of the goals of a Hindu state with no restrictions whatsoever. The result would be an expulsion of non-Hindu Indians out of its borders to facilitate which many would in turn be injured. All of this will happen without any questions being raised.

Now back to reality. India, despite it being home to a wide palette of cultures and religions, remains a victim of religious fundamentalism. However the fact that it is a democracy (although a really flawed one), does account for a restriction against blatant extremism.

However this does not really answer the question above, but the following, hopefully shall. It is difficult for any nation, having had a taste for democracy, to regress into a non-inclusive institution. The same is the case with India. Mr. Modi may have won the elections by a larger margin (via electoral hacking or other means…), however this does not mean that he behaves undemocratically. To the contrary, he knows very well than others that any attempt to make India undemocratic would simply raise Indians against him. He may suppress them in the short term, but this would simply raise many more in contempt. In a nation with a population of over a billion, I believe that the power finally is with the people. Mr. Modi and his party may via political clout and deception have certain measures to shut dissent, but there is always a threshold for everything, and this threshold lowers as the populace experiences a certain level of freedom (as a democracy provides).

Lets now address yet another crucial question: **If we are transitioning to a better world, then how does one explain the rise in the number of protests all over the world in authoritarianisms and democracies alike?**

Countering this question would require us to understand the essence of any protest, the core of which is dissatisfaction and frustration. Thus the direct relation of protest and discontent leads one to the conclusion of a rise in discontent over the years, since the numbers of protests have increased. Thus, leading us to an apocryphal conclusion of greater suffering today than in the past; ipso facto monarchies must have been better than democracies.

I would, however beg to differ - every protest has yet another nuanced underpinning to its existence, one of dissent, defiance and rejection; all of which require courage and faith, which in turn build up as one feels the need to unshackle oneself from conformism and admonish the rulers on one's right to freedom. In addition to this dynamic of every protest, the openness and inclusivity of an institution further plays an enhancing role in the manifestation of the aforementioned courage and faith. From this stream of logic, one can thus conclusively argue that the rise in the number of protests is also an indication of a society becoming more open and inclusive. To supplement this with an analogy - not longer than a century ago swathes of Indians marched in unison to gain independence from their colonizers, yet today they protest in smaller numbers for an issue that may seem petty when placed in comparison to independence. For the freedom fighters, independence was of prime importance and was an issue which could gather numbers to startle the British; had they gathered a few hundreds of Indians and marched against the felling of trees (the 'Chipko Andolan' which happened much later), they would have most certainly been massacred, as seen at the 'Jallianwala Bagh'. Yet today, even fewer Indians can march in protest against an issue as petty as allowing outside food in cinema halls, and they get the necessary media attention necessary; their success maybe short term, however keeping the results aside, what is important is that their concerns received due coverage by the media and have been addressed by the state authorities too. The aggravated may not have received all they desired, but they received due consideration, the latter being important in a democracy; after all not everyone can have all they desire, which is why democracy represents a compromise, as Shashi Tharoor brilliantly put it - "It is all fine as long as we can agree on how to disagree!". All of this is to say that one should not look at a protest as something in itself, but link it to a larger cycle, one which is inherent in a democracy; an evolution of societal existence within the framework of a democracy.

Education, literacy and experience (of which historical precedents from a critical basis) are auxiliary forces which can help explain the evolutionary dynamic talked about above.

Over the years literacy has increased exponentially and so have protests:

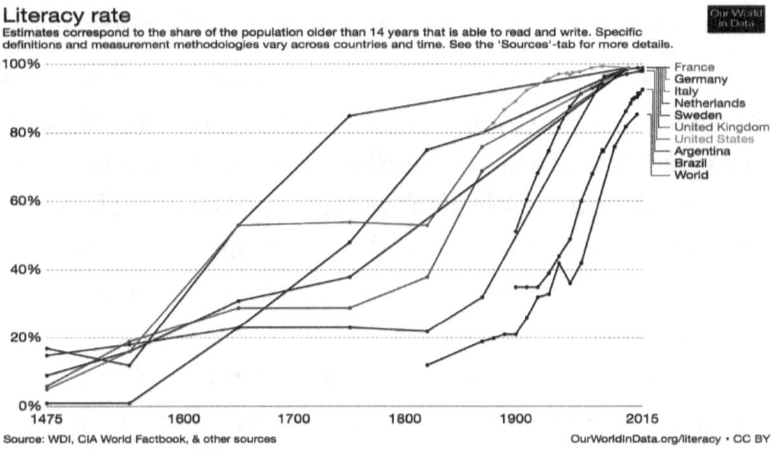

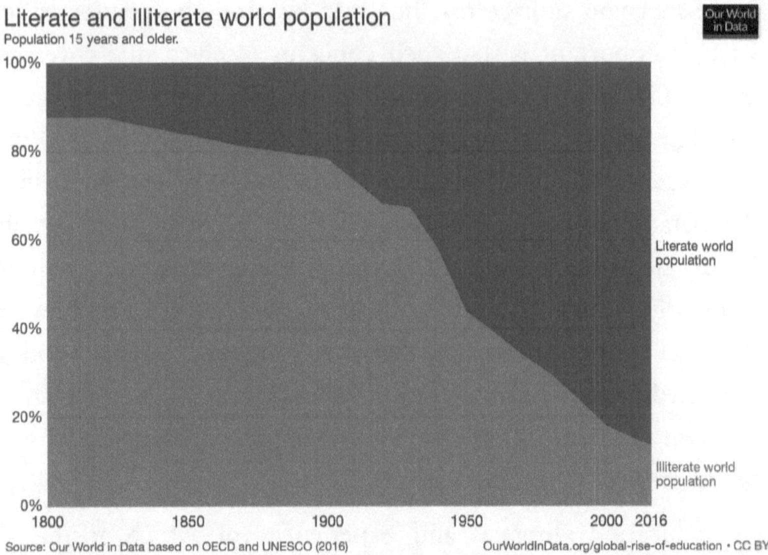

The relation between literacy and protests is relatively easy to explain with the former increasing awareness, which in turn facilitates the realization of power within oneself. It is precisely because of this dynamic that developed countries tend to have strong checks and balances in comparison to undeveloped ones.

Going back to the initial question, when the numbers of protests are used to show a measure of dissatisfaction and hence the failure of a system, we fail take into account the numbers of suppressed protests. Why don't we have equal number of protests in North Korea? Is it because the system there is a wonderful success? Quite to contrary, the system there is the worst failure; frequent famines and starvation haunt the residents, whilst propaganda seeks to crush and minimize dissent as well as change. North Korea is by no measure a "happy place" but is in fact one where protests are suppressed by their ruler. Does this however mean that North Korea is destined to remain an oppressed failed state? Not really; as I mentioned earlier frustration cannot be bottled forever and North Koreans will one day fulminate. Many scholars are seeing signs of an uprising of the 'Arab Spring' magnitude. History is evidence that people do find a way to fight against extractive institutions, reinstating power amongst themselves in the process. This was explained by Karl Marx in his theory of *"Dialectical Materialism"*.

The future for North Korea is uncertain, just as it was for the 'Arab Spring Countries' wherein Tunisia went on to proclaim democratic status, whereas Egypt fell prey to the clutches of despotism. Regardless of whether, in the short-term, North Korea becomes a democracy or remains an authoritarian regime, we need to keep in mind that change is an ongoing process and any systemic change cannot be realized with a single uprising. An uprising, indeed is a sign of an abrupt movement in the stream of change, yet there is always more to come. If North Korea does become an inclusive state like Tunisia, there is cause for celebration. If it ends up like Egypt, hope is not lost, for with time people will find a way to overcome extractive institutions, much like the Indian scenario which attained independence a century after its first independence movement. I, for one, do not believe that protests are mere outbursts of frustration, unconnected with one another. Their success or failure should not be quantified on the basis of their immediate results. It is an integral element of a 'learning curve' forming an inherent equilibrium mechanism within societal existence, persistently pushing us to a desirable mode of existence.

When protests are suppressed, the result often is a massive uprising of the magnitude of the Arab Spring. Russia is expecting something similar and so is North Korea. The revolutions and uprisings of the past can be considered to be symptomatic of the same. Thus when we notice a large number of smaller protests and a negligible number of mass uprisings one could theorize the transition toward a **relatively** open world, which doesn't bottle every frustration. In fact our leaders are bound to have learned a little something from the past: the fact that preventing protests would merely end as an outburst large enough to cause an institutional overhaul, much to any tyrant's detriment.

Is democracy a universal institution?

In my opinion, it may not be a perfect institution, but it certainly is the best of all alternatives we have. Its superiority lies in its fundamental advantages of freedom of expression, right to dissent and most importantly anti-incumbency. These are advantages that no alternative structure accommodates. As the renowned author and economist Amartya Sen mentions in his book *"The Argumentative Indian"*, the great strength of India over China (despite the economic superiority of the latter) lay in its voice as a democracy; today if President Xi decides to eliminate a section of the populace, no one can dare to question his will, worse yet no one would probably know before the deed is done; on the other hand an action of similar cruelty would be impossible in a democracy like India.

A democracy should provide unbridled freedom of expression, irrefutable right to dissent and most importantly furnish pristine sovereignty to the people. Clearly, these provisions remain absent in praxis, however we do see shades of the same. These shades, though tarnished, remain far superior to the total paucity of such virtues in non-democratic institutions. I don't think I need to delve into the importance of these virtues as scholars have for centuries expounded on their unrivalled benefits.

Despite these advantages, the question of its universalism remains untouched. To put it rather more simplistically: is a democracy as viable in a homogenous nation as it is in a pluralistic one? Justifying the existence of a democracy in a pluralist nation is no herculean task. Congenial coexistence of multiple races, creeds, customs, religions, languages, costumes and cuisines form the very basis of pluralism. This basis can survive only in a democratic setup, wherein equality to every individual provides dignified defence to ones culture and heritage. In an authoritarian regime, where chances are that the dictator has risen to power on communal and sectarian grounds in the very first place, the nation turns hostile against pluralist ideas and ideologues which threaten the superiority of the majoritarian community. To put it slightly differently, a democracy is born out of pluralism, whereas authoritarianism is born out of communalism which requires impairing pluralism in the process.

Having defended the importance of democracy in a pluralistic setup, how about a homogenous setup. It is indubitably true that in a community that shares the same culture, custom, costume and cuisine (which is highly unlikely in the modern 'diasporic' world) people would unlikely get into feuds, however even then it is important to shield opinions and individualism. In fact the most homogenous communities suffered suppression because often a few of differing mindsets succumbed to the majoritarian view. Whether a democracy or an authoritarian regime would work with greater efficacy in a homogenous society is debatable, however if the latter does win the cause, it shall be at the cost of intellectual freedom, which for me is of greater importance. Primitive India is a clear example of a homogenous society thriving under the power of the 'Brahmin' (priests).

Even though each village/society/community within themselves shared the same religion, language and beliefs, they more gravely demarcated on the basis of the caste system. The caste system, which rooted prejudice and inequality in Indian society, led to the plundering of lower castes to enrich the educated priesthood. Even in a homogenous society, with people in authority acting in congruence to acceptable social norms and for shared social needs, a chunk of the populace found itself scathed by the cruelty of the system. It would only be much later in a democratic India, that the lower castes (Dalits) could voice their concerns, be heard and uplift themselves gradually; so much so that we had a Dalit Member of Parliament (Mayawati) and several political parties addressing their concerns.

Even today, if a homogenous society finds itself under authoritarianism, the predicament would be similar to primitive India, the only difference being the manifestation of the caste-system as the infamous class-system. This is not to say that class inequality is absent in democracies. Quite to the contrary, economic inequality is as perverse in democracies as it is in a military rule.

I have often heard several Indians express their desire for a dictator who should rectify all the foibles of the Indian democracy who would, once the changes are in place, hand over the reign back to a democracy. What they desire is a benevolent dictator. This idea seems really ludicrous to me. The benevolence of a dictator is not something that comes as a guarantee or assurance, in fact it is a gift based purely on luck. No one knew that Lee Kuan Kew was destined to be a benevolent dictator, it was only during and after his extremely beneficial term that Singapore praised his efforts. Having witnessed a series of exploitative and theocratic Mughal emperors, no one would have expected Akbar to be a man with pluralistic and rational ideologies. In fact Akbar, a devout Muslim, made efforts to initiate a new religion *'Rah-i-Akl'*, one based on reason (Rah - path, Akl - reason: path of reason), taking the good points from all religions and amalgamating them into one religion, devoid of prejudice. Akbar's courts were renowned for the wide representation each belief and community received, even the atheists. All of this to say, receiving a benevolent dictator is not a choice, but a gift and hoping that the next dictator will be one is a massive gamble, the odds of which tilt clearly in the favour of the likes of Hitler and Mussolini.

In addition to this gamble, another fallacy in this 'desire' is of the assumption that a despot would willingly hand over power to the people, once his job is done. Yet another ironic aspect is that of interestingly 'electing' a dictator, which I think is self-explanatory of the gaffe in such a preposterous desire.

A few have made 'Brexit' as a highlight of the failure of democracy, stating that the near equal numbers of Brits for and against leaving the European Union. The referendum in my opinion is a sign of strength; a sign of democracy in action. Someone told the other day that the result which would be on the side of 51% would leave the 49% in dire discontent, which is a failure of democracy. In my opinion, if the regime was an non-democratic one, then the 49% would never have known that they are a massive 49%; the 49% would have never had their opinions heard; who knows if the people in power belonged to the 49%, then they may have even won, pushing a majority into accepting something they would have perhaps have not even had a chance to express their discontent for. Many state that democracies often neglect minorities and flow with a majoritarian choice, which is truly the way the structure is framed, however would the issue be any better in a non-democratic regime? I seriously doubt so. First, in a democracy, the minorities also have certain fundamental rights, in accordance with which a majoritarian view may be carried out.

Moreover, often democracies like India have been structured in a way that for a political party to come to power, they have to acknowledge the existence of minorities by processing their demands. To the contrary, in a non-democratic structure, especially one built on communal and sectarian grounds, minorities are more often than not driven out in order to maintain homogeneity (which is in itself a political tactic to prevent dissent). The case of Tibet, China and Buddhism is a classic example; with the Dalai Lama and other Buddhist adherents having to flee Tibet in fear of the much mightier communist China.

This is again not to say that minorities are always respected in democracies. India, a land of contradictions, shall again serve as a great example. The largest democracy in the world, with our current Prime Minster, linked to perhaps one of the most non-democratic deeds in contemporary Indian history, the infamous "Gujarat riots", wherein several Muslims (minorities) were slaughtered. Where is the democracy I so loyally preached of in the previous paragraph. Honestly, it is absent and there exists no justification for what was done. The only argument one could advance in defence of a democracy is perhaps that the Modi wave in India is one based on farcical rhetoric, which has been successfully persuasive primarily because the 'democratic pillars' I stated in the beginning aren't quite as strong as they should be.

Flaws do exist in democracies, for instance fundamentalism and sectarianism in India, but if we were to take to an authoritarian regime, then these ailments would simply be amplified and not suppressed. The only way these issues would perhaps be solved in non-democracies is if the minorities are wiped out in entirety.

"Democracy has institutionalized divisions." This is a statement quite true in its claim, however need not necessarily be interpreted as an impediment. I believe that institutionalizing the differences has gone a long way to help minorities and fringe groups acknowledge as well as bolster their beliefs, claims and demands. Institutionalizing differences need not be seen as a negative, which makes a country more divisive, but can indeed be seen as the modus operandi to empowering overshadowed beliefs and ideologies. Countries all over the world, India included, are today more diverse than ever. Such diversity is never gifted with an equal power and number balance between every community within. In India, for instance, Parsis were always and still are a minority however for them institutionalizing differences wasn't all that advantageous, primarily because they were never really under oppression. At the same time 'Dalits' in India, though in numbers much larger than Parsis, were victims of callous discrimination and oppression; for this underprivileged community, the institutionalizing of differences, further augmented by political parties whose manifestos revolved around 'a Dalit's needs', has come a long way in mitigating the deep-dyed power imbalance created over centuries of prejudiced existence.

India boasts of its diversity and pluralism, and this pluralism, I believe, is not under threat due to institutionalizing of differences. Quite to the contrary, the unhindered acknowledgement of differences in social and political spheres has helped India develop a ground for consensus despite the multifarious cultural disposition of our country. To quote Shashi Tharoor (a world renowned historian, author and Indian politician), the pith of a pluralist democracy is in its ability to " agree on the ground rules on how to disagree", for which one must have an understanding of differences in the very first place. Tharoor also mentions in one of his speeches that India (much like any pluralist entity) is not a melting pot, but is in fact much like an Indian 'Thali', a tasty variety of dishes and vegetables all placed in the same plate yet separated from each other; each dish is as important as any other and has its unique traits, however when amalgamated like a melting pot, every dish loses its unique flavour and the *'Thali'* is outstripped of its vibrance.

The *'Thali'* is a classic analogy linking the importance of differences to the uniqueness of dishes and also highlighting the importance of unity using the vibrance of the plate in its entirety. To catechize this paragraph, Institutionalized divisions facilitate acknowledgment of differences and enable us to rally around a consensus despite our differences. This is not to say that a society without Institutionalized divisions would be unable to do so; the focal flaw in such a scenario however would be the minority (not only by numbers, but also power) remaining camouflaged in the guise of other opinions, beliefs and ideologies simply, to prevent social rejection or disapproval.

It is an undeniable fact that democratic institutions often emerged out of capitalism. Raghuram Rajan in his book *"The Third Pillar"* explains the same with great dexterity. However it would be wrong to assume that either is non-existent in the absence of the other. In other words, democracy can function even in the absence of capitalism. Pre-liberalization India is an example. "Socialist democracies" if at all feasible would certainly tackle the problems associated with rampant capitalism, however at the same time would perhaps have flaws of its own. Neo-liberal capitalism is what plagues the world today and people like to believe that the same is the reason behind the emergence of democratic constructs. It is most certainly difficult to gun down this belief, however at the same time let's not confine the two as inseparable components.

A democracy is in general always a slower process than its alternatives. Discussion clearly takes longer than one man calling the shots. If Hitler perhaps had an unbiased panel of democratically elected ministers, then Hitler's murderous ideas would have perhaps worn out with discussion (which takes time). In the end it boils down to one's priorities. Would one prefer a freer and representative system at the cost of fast-tracked decision making? I most certainly would (and many would perhaps share my priority) not only because freedom is sacrosanct to me, but also because 'quick-decision' making can more than often translate into 'rash-decision' making; the Great Leap Forward and the Cultural Revolution are exemplary of the same.

I shall now end by quoting Mohandas Karamchand Gandhi, the Father of India -

> **"Democracy is something that gives the weak the same chance as the strong."**

This statement is indubitably far from reality, however its importance must not be undermined. As we embark on a journey where every critical juncture is under scrutiny (as it should be; in fact a true democratic believer would rejoice in such scrutiny), let us not discard every system that isn't quixotic. We need to study its existence (flawed as it may be) parallel to its alternatives and then perhaps grasp its importance in history, and for ages to come.

4

Anonymity on the Internet: Shield or Weapon?

As we debate the freedom of expression, it is important to understand the internet is also a medium of expression for many and assuring anonymity enables them with the freedom they desire. However this freedom comes with hateful and false information floating around the internet. As such discussing whether anonymity on the internet is a shield or a weapon becomes vital.

(This piece was co-written by Anirudh Choudhury as part of a competition organized at Jai Hind College.)

This piece was completed on the 18ᵗʰ of September, 2019.

"I believe in absolute freedom of expression.
Everyone has a right to offend and to be offended."

– Taslima Nasreen

Free speech is the foundation of our liberties and throughout history, we've argued passionately about issues, beliefs, ideas and policies. It's not always pretty - but the right to say what we believe and to publish those beliefs has been an essential part of liberty. The idea of anonymity has prevailed since Shakespearian times with Shakespeare itself being a pseudonym wherein several literary figures used nom de plume or total anonymity to shift the focus on the content rather than themselves. Anonymity has existed in the form of a platform for individuals to express ideologies often contradicting the majoritarian point of view; discussing particularly volatile, sensitive and personal subjects. Anonymity on the internet is premised on a similar rationale and therefore banning an ideology that has persisted since ages(for the greater good) seems quite irrational, unjustifiable, ludicrous and almost self-serving.

True that non-anonymity keeps a check on the way one expresses oneself on the internet but it also makes themselves vulnerable to personal attacks like doxing, swatting and revenge porn. However the concept of anonymity is also important in scenarios that aren't as serious or even more serious as the ones mentioned above. Military communications require maximum security. Even with secure encryption, a lot of information can be obtained from just the packet headers by professional hackers. Hence, the commanders, officers, and field agents of military use anonymity. Military personnel require anonymous communications to protect themselves and their strategies from terrorist attacks. All communications during the killing of Osama

Bin Laden had been kept behind a veil. Financial institutions participate in security clearing houses on a daily basis. They use online anonymity to safeguard their data since it is possible that the security of one financial institution could be breached leading to overall compromise on data security. Investment bankers protect their investment decisions by operating anonymously and escaping from snoopers.

Some might say that the world would be a better place if we were all held accountable for what and how we express on the internet but real-name policies reduce some (but not most) offensive speech, but they also deter people from contributing thoughtfully to controversial topics. Many of the strongest arguments for anonymous speech were made by the NAACP (National Association for the Advancement of Coloured People) and other dissidents in the 1950s and 1960s. Their political opponents wanted to obtain their names in order to retaliate against them. Sometimes anonymity allows us to speak the unpopular truth. Without any anonymity the revelation of high stake secrets would also come with serious consequences. Edward Snowden blew the whistle on the NSA's (National Security Agency) collaborations with foreign and domestic agencies to monitor the activities of American citizens anonymously, yet on revealing his identity was pressed with several charges. Similarly Jullian Assange the founder of "WikiLeaks" never stepped out of the Ecuadorian embassy in London in lieu of being arrested. He would have been a free man today had he remained anonymous; living in a box is his reward for revealing the truth.

Anonymity is an underlying yet significant component of our societal structure, which remains unavoidable. Anonymous communication can be achieved in real life by sharing/posting an unsigned letter or calling a person anonymously. The majority of users taking advantage of anonymous services on the internet, deem them to be truly necessary and specific in terms of their ability to satisfy a need.

Banning anonymity is escapism at its best. Evading a problem instead of confronting it, by eliminating an entire platform, which for many, is a venue to express themselves freely and fearlessly, is really no solution. It's no different from abolishing the right of an author to compose, as a result of the works of a particular author, which is in its core a flawed decision.

Salman Rushdie's controversial *"Satanic Verses"*, which was banned in India in 1988, had significant ripple effects on other authors who consequently refrained from working on literary works that diverted and digressed from the majoritarian view. Now would we want to climb down the ladder of liberty and freedom by banning anonymity which is analogous to banning the freedom of speech.

The availability of the technology to set up such an anonymous server also makes the elimination of such servers virtually impossible; one is created, as soon as another is shut down. The need to forge an identity or use another person's identity to correspond anonymously is eliminated given the current availability of such services. People on the net are anonymous to some degree anyway because of the inherent characteristics of the medium for it is one of the basis of its existence. Services providing additional anonymity are only expanding on this feature of the net.

The impact of an anonymity ban can lead to a contemporary fascist structure wherein power, through greater knowledge of our personal details, can be used to restrict and establish near absolute control over the masses. Given our history of corruption who's to say this wouldn't be parallel to the lines ushering into a subtle dictatorial setup, which in our socially-capitalist, ever evolving and globalizing economy would be devastating.

It is true that with the freedom of expression comes in a range of problems, yet these problems aren't unique to the internet. Unpopular speech is a necessary/obvious consequence of free speech and it was widely accepted long ago, during the drafting of the Constitution and the Bill of Rights, that the advantages of free speech clearly outweigh its disadvantages. This is a fundamental principle on and off the internet. The fact remains that more than 15,000 email messages are sent anonymously each day which display the significance of anonymous services on the net. The wish for internet remaining unregulated seems rather naïve. Attempts to artificially eliminate this service through legislation would not be right in terms of efficiency and ethicality. If anonymity is truly a negative, it will naturally die out from a lack of use.

5

Climate Change - Sparking the World's Largest Refugee Crisis

Climate Change is an incredibly important global issue and an anthology of essays without a piece on it would be incomplete. Thus as the last essay in this book, we discuss how climate change is potentially resulting in the largest refugee crisis in the world today.

(This piece is a publication of evolvideas, an LLP which seeks to spread ideas and empower thought. I am privileged to be a founder member of this wonderful organization. The co-writers of this specific piece are Rajat Roy, Neelkabir Varsha Kapil and Shania, all of whom are dear friends and founder members of evolvideas.)

This piece was completed on the 25th of October, 2019.

"The fitness of a biological species can only be determined by their ability to evolve according to their changing environment" - a statement printed across biology textbooks, in some form or another, as a part of Darwin's groundbreaking evolutionary theory. But, what if, for the first time in this world's history, a species decides to abdicate its home planet as a result of the very actions it mindlessly proliferated across the world? Human settlements on Mars may well be the only hope for the continuity of our species; a possible reality by the year 2031. That very year, however, rings the death-knell for the Earth. Twelve years, just slightly more than a decade, until we bid farewell to bejewelled pristine oceans, and dense and lush forests. Twelve years until we must reconcile with arid desert, or fateful floods. Twelve years, until the Earth sees an environmental Armageddon: one that's already begun; one that has led to the creation of refugees fleeing due to climate change.

Our species has already begun running; to drier land, to higher ground, and to cleaner, safer zones against the fury of Mother Nature. Dear Climate Migrants: your fight is only beginning. The term 'Climate Migrant' or 'Climate Refugee' is used to refer to an individual who is forced to flee from their place of residence as a result of sudden or gradual changes in the natural environment around them, due to rising sea levels, extremities in the weather or draught and consequently famine. Now, 259 years after man powered the first machines, the effects of the Industrial Revolution are being felt by individuals in less developed countries, who are being forced to abandon their homes and their livelihood just to be able to live.

The Modern World, with it, ushered in a whole new era. An era of incessant and discriminate use of coal and fossil fuels, an era with clouds of gas looming over us, an era with acid rain, an era where the harbingers of the Modern World has now denounced its very end. Indeed, 259 years after man's cruelly ingenious utilization of coal to power heavy machinery, we have begun to bear the consequences. With our current carbon dioxide (CO_2) levels reaching historic 'highs' since the Earth's inception, and multiple cities around the world being ranked as extremely polluted, it's no surprise that the planet is fighting back. The oceans are growing stronger, deeper, more powerful; the glorious polar ice-caps irreversibly melting, carrying away thousands of species that have survived millennia of peace only to be wiped away in a tsunami of careless fury. It's no wonder that humans too, as a species, are beginning to face the same fate.

The end of the world, or their world at least, is something the people of Maldives experience firsthand every single day. Seeing an annual rise of a whopping 12 millimetres of ocean per year, and the disappearance of eight of the Micronesian Islands, much like the Marshall Islands, Maldivians can only lie in wait to embrace their apocalyptic fate, taking solace in knowing that multiple other countries, such as Haiti, Kenya and Papua New Guinea, bear earthquakes, cyclones, and high tides regularly; their residents trusting their heels, in the fulfilment of a primal instinct: survival. With a plethora of Haitian refugees quickly fleeing to the United States, the Dominican Republic, the Bahamas, Argentina and Chile, it seems as though the climate change catastrophe is finally leading to a global refugee crisis.

The problem, rather than simply feeding socio-humanitarian journals and filling up their pages with images of teary and distraught migrants, is also despairingly turning into a bureaucratic nightmare. Under the 1951 Geneva Convention relating to the status of refugees – which has covered political and war refugees – environmental migrants can find no respite to their woes. In addition, the United Nations High Commission for Refugees, and the United Nations' Development Programme are wary of introducing this new category into the definition of a "refugee" or "migrant". In reaching full capacity in handling 22.5 million political and war related refugees, adding this new clause will certainly lead to explosive results for these organizations; the refugee crisis will then, officially, spiral out of control and a world becoming increasingly more "nationalistic" provides no solace.

While the depth and the breadth of information on Global Warming, and our 12-year window of correction seems as inexhaustible as the depth of the Marianas Trench (which is also home to a horde of plastics and non-biodegradable waste), even through our conscious efforts, we are unable to extinguish the use of plastics; the burning of fossil fuels; the leaching of chemicals into soil from hazardous waste: all to satisfy our comfortable way of existence. Climate Change is no longer an abstract concept that we read in our science textbooks, but a reality in the lives of people worldwide. Pollution is real. Fluctuating temperatures, toxic gases, rising sea levels, the extinction of nearly one-eighth of all our species is an increasing threat that looms over our heads every day. Their blood, their death and our dismemberment are on our hands.

It's often said that "ignorance is bliss" - that the constant denial of a particular concept or action leads to psychological stability. Climate Change, however, with its stellar and unshakeable evidence, is one concept that should not, could not and dare not be denied. Especially not by leaders who hold the key to modern day society. Indeed, by altogether denying the existence of climate change - "The concept of Global Warming was created by and for the Chinese in order to make the U.S. manufacturing non-competitive" (Twitter, @realDonaldTrump, 6 Nov 2012) - and then proceeding to have a teenage on-again, off-again relationship with this concept through famously controversial statements is of no help; "I don't believe it" and "It'll change back". Denying millions of graphs, some produced by the government's very own environmental agencies that have shown a steady rise in CO2 emissions citing the 2010 atmospheric levels to be nearly 31 billion tonnes, is not going to flip a switch in the heavens and cause the reversal of this catastrophe.

Surely, deporting Haitian migrants desperately in need of a new home and ignoring the imminent extinction of multiple common species such as giraffes or penguins will not cause this crisis to simply fade away. These animals are just as much climate refugees as the people. Are we really going to sacrifice our precious pale, blue dot, for the want of a comfortable life; plaguing the atmosphere with smoke and dust and dirt, and infusing the seas with millions of tonnes of plastic each year, choking marine life and creating plastic islands larger than France in the Pacific Ocean? Is suicidal genocide through climate change really what we want to be remembered for: a world where water is more expensive than gasoline.

Charity begins at home: let us put into action these simple, proverbial statements we so ardently preach, and illustriously revere, with respect to saving our planet, and the lives of our own brothers and sisters. Individual choice, individual foray into this sector, and individual changes, can truly impact the oceans; impact the air; impact the land, and impact the lives of our fellow human beings, thousands of kilometres away. After all, we're in this together. We're not in a race against each other, we're in a race to rectify our ancestral actions. Rather than abusing the Earth and ensuring a front-row seat to the apocalypse, let us try to conserve the sapphire blue jewel of this night sky: it's the only one we have.

We, as a species, hold the power to rebuild or destroy the planet. The fate of 8.7 million other species depends on it. Let us, together, take a stand against the ghost we ourselves have created instead of simply disregarding its existence and pretending that the world turns safely on its deathbed. Let us use these 12 years: which may seem like much to us, but is less than the blink of an eye in the cosmic timeline - to save our planet and the 8.7 million species on it. Only if we can change ourselves, our ways, our ideas and face the problem, we shall endure.

"Alone we can do so little, together we can do so much."

Acknowledgments

A very special thanks to my teachers and my school for having shaped me and moulded me in every way possible.

A very special thanks to my college and the faculty for having exposed me to boundaries that I didn't expect to explore so soon in life.

Most importantly an incredibly special thanks to my grandfather and mother for having pushed me to publish this small collection of essays.

A very special thanks to all my role models, to name a few, Dr. Amartya Sen, Dr. Raghuram Rajan, Dr. Shashi Tharoor, Dr. Ramachandra Guha and my dear mentor/father figure Mr. David Cecil

THANK YOU

You can send your feedback at aditbiha12345@gmail.com